Jim

Keep the baseball tradition alive

Jim Halloran

BASEBALL AND AMERICA

JIM HALLORAN

"Whoever wants to know the
heart and mind of America had
better learn baseball."

trimarkpress

LIBRARY OF CONGRESS CATALOGING-IN-PUBLICATION DATA

BASEBALL AND AMERICA
JIM HALLORAN

P. CM.

ISBN: 978-1-943401-49-9
LIBRARY OF CONGRESS CONTROL NUMBER: 2018956791

I-18
10 9 8 7 6 5 4 3 2 1
FIRST EDITION
PRINTED AND BOUND IN THE UNITED STATES OF AMERICA

A PUBLICATION OF TRIMARK PRESS, INC.
368 SOUTH MILITARY TRAIL
DEERFIELD BEACH, FL 33442
800.889.0693
WWW.TRIMARKPRESS.COMTA

DEDICATION

Baseball and America is dedicated to my
four wonderful grandchildren –
Henry, Gavin, Jane and Lydia,
and to all the other children
and grandchildren of future generations
with the hope they, too, will learn
the value that baseball can add to
their relationships with friends and family.

Acknowledgements

A sincere thank you goes out to all who have given assistance and support to this book. The hard working staff at Trimark Press — Barry, Lorie and Christelle, worked tirelessly editing and formatting the book.

Patrick Yost, owner and editor of the Morgan County Citizen newspaper, published the initial attempts of writing the manuscript. I am grateful to Lisa Moss for her part in the initial editing and formatting of the book, and to Danielle Hawkins for assisting in the cover and back cover design.

I appreciate the gang of 23 reviewers who offered suggestions and provided support. The story contributors, Pedro, Les, Tim, Mike, Jack, Frank, and Rob told their great tales of baseball.

Sean Holtz of the fabulous Baseball Almanac provided much needed assistance in the gathering of data and photos. Reginald Howard, Jr., veteran of the Negro Leagues and a fine gentleman, shared his views on the Negro Leagues. Dr. Raymond Roswell of the Negro League Museum generously provided photos of Negro League ballplayers.

Linda Peek Schacht graciously donated the art work of her late husband Mike Schacht.

Thank you, Mark Schlabach, Mike Nabors, and Steve Hertz, for taking the time to read the material and offering your endorsement comments on the back cover.

And last, but certainly not least, I am grateful for the proof reading skills and patience provided by my wife of 52 years, Diane.

TABLE OF CONTENTS

INTRODUCTION

A Tie That Binds

Gather 'round parents, grandparents and teachers with your children and students to take a journey through the 150 years of baseball and how it has mirrored our country's history and bonded generations of families. Baseball has tied generation to generation and adult to child like no other sport or cultural experience. We see it in the passing along of folk lore stories of players such as Babe Ruth and Satchel Paige. We see how it has brought together cities and entire regions of the country when celebrating their team victories. We see how it has brought together the citizens of our country and helped lead us out of despair when enduring extreme hardships such as 9/11. Along with the country, baseball has confronted racial discrimination and labor problems. It has suffered through the pains of war and the ups and downs of economic cycles. The USA is attached to the sport of baseball.

For older generations, the history outlined here will refresh many life events and bring a touch of nostalgia. For the newer fan, the pairing of history and baseball will add to the enjoyment of the game and provide a renewed appreciation for our country's history. For the student it will introduce a sport that will be with you for the rest of your life.

The best way to read *Baseball and America* will be with a laptop or a digital tablet close by in order to explore with a click any subject that piques your interest for more information.

Better yet, read it with a fellow fan. It is bound to create fun conversation and may lead to taking in a game together at a nearby professional, college, or high school baseball field.

In The Beginning

Civil War hero Abner Doubleday (1819-1893) was incorrectly named as the founder of American baseball by a commission headed by National League President Abraham Mills in 1907. The Doubleday myth was actually started by Al Spalding, former star pitcher and baseball club executive, as a method to ensure that the game was cited as purely American and not just a spinoff from the British game of cricket. This baseball myth is responsible for the National Baseball Hall of Fame choosing Cooperstown, New York as its location; Abner Doubleday spent his high school days in Cooperstown. Although later discredited as the inventor of baseball, Doubleday is noted in history for firing the first shot in the opening battle of the Civil War at Fort Sumter. Doubleday went on to become a famous Union General.

I t was the 1870s and America had entered its "age of enterprise." The Civil War was in the past and reconstruction efforts were well under way. We were becoming an industrialized economy on the verge of creating wealth as never considered possible. Over the next 15 years output of manufactured goods would increase 150 percent and per capita income would rise by 50 percent over the same period of time. The transcontinental railroad, the steel industry and the grass roots of the oil industry were leading the way. Andrew Carnegie founded US Steel, John D. Rockefeller created the Standard Oil Company, Cornelius Vanderbilt was the leader in building the railroad industry, and Cyrus McCormick created the reaper. Thomas Edison invented the light bulb, and Alexander Graham Bell the telephone. They were the Steven Jobs and Bill Gates of their time, leading the way into a new era of technology.

The Great Western Movement was continuing along with the war against Native American Indians. Back east the newspapers were telling the story of General George Custer's demise by Sitting Bull at the Massacre at Little Big Horn. Indians were being forced into reservations and eventually their children into white man schools to learn the way of the white man. Buffalo Bill's Wild West Show featuring Buffalo Bill Cody and Annie Oakley became a big hit in the East and the West.

Rutherford Hayes had replaced Ulysses S. Grant as

President. He sat gloriously in the White House, witnessing this robust economic era. Lurking in the background, however, was labor unrest and violence.

Enter professional baseball — a product of entrepreneurs in this age of enterprise. Baseball was not new. It had been around in some form or another for fifty years. Originally it was adapted from the English game of cricket which was played with a wicket, a ball, and divided into innings. Later it was transformed into rounder or town ball, a game played with a stick and ball and a home plate to count runs. The rudimentary form of the game was played during the Civil War at encampments of union and confederate soldiers. Amateur teams were formed in towns and villages across the country and townspeople turned out in droves to watch the games. As an early indication of baseball in America, Abraham Lincoln enjoyed playing the game and it was rumored that he was playing the game when he was informed that he had won the presidential nomination in 1860. A political cartoon in 1860 depicts Abraham Lincoln holding the winning ball in his presidential campaign against four candidates.

The National Game. Three Outs and One Run (1860). Published by Currier & Ives. A pro-Lincoln satire, deposited for copyright weeks before the 1860 presidential election. The contest is portrayed as a baseball game in which Lincoln has defeated (left to right) John Bell, Stephen A. Douglas, and John C. Breckinridge. Source: Library of Congress.

The Civil War brought more attention to what was then a rough version of baseball. Both Union and Confederate troops found it as a much needed morale booster and boredom distraction. Using whatever was available that could be transformed into bats and balls baseball became the major entertainment of encampments.

In researching an article written for Baseball Almanac, Author Michael Aubrecht found letters sent home that described baseball at the camps. Private Alpheris B. Parker of the 10th Massachusetts wrote, " The parade ground has been a busy place for a week or so past, ball-playing having become a mania in camp. Officers and men forget, for a time, the differences in rank and indulge in the invigorating sport with a school boy's ardor."

Another private writing home from Virginia recalled, "It is astonishing how indifferent a person can become to danger. The report of musketry is heard but a very little distance from us…yet over there on the other side of the road most of our company, playing bat ball and perhaps in less than half an hour, they may be called to play a Ball game of a more serious

Sam Crawford (1880–1968)
Played 19 years as an outfielder with
Cincinnati and Detroit, starting in 1898.
Inducted into the Hall of Fame in 1957.

"I remember as a teenager when I made my first team baseball trip. A bunch of us made a trip overland in a wagon drawn by a team of horses. We started out and went from town to town playing their teams.

"One of the boys was a coronet player and when we'd come into a town he'd whip out that coronet and sound off. We'd announce that we were the Wahoo team and were ready for a ball game. We didn't have any uniforms or anything, just baseball shoes, maybe, but we had a manager. It wasn't easy to win those games because every town had its own umpire. We were gone three or four weeks. Lived on bread and beefsteak. We'd sleep anywhere. Sometimes in a tent, lots of time on the ground out in the open."

— Excerpt from an interview in 1966,
(Glory of Our Times)

Source: Dyja, Thomas. "America's Rites of Passage," Civil War Times Illustrated, Harrisburg, Pa.

nature."

George Putnam, a Union soldier wrote with humor a story of a game being called early due to a surprise attack on their camp by Confederate infantry." Suddenly there was a scattering of fire, which three outfielders caught the brunt; the centerfield was hit and was captured, left and right field managed to get back to our lines. The attack...was rejected without serious difficulty, but we had lost not only our centerfielder, but .... the only baseball in Alexandria, Texas."

Rise of Professional Baseball Clubs

It should come as no surprise that entrepreneurs would come up with a business plan to make money out of this popular pastime. There were at least two attempts by player groups to form a professional baseball league in the early 1870s but they failed due to a lack of resources and discipline. But in 1876 a group of investors formed the eight team National League of Professional Baseball Clubs. The new league was able to recruit the two most well known players of its time, second baseman "Cap" Anson and pitcher Al Spalding and somehow held together. It was reasonably well organized, properly financed, and most importantly, controlled the players by creation of the reserve clause which bound the players to a particular team or owner for their entire career unless traded to another owner. The eight team league consisted of Chicago, St. Louis, Hartford, Boston, Louisville, New York, Philadelphia and Cincinnati. The Cincinnati Red Stockings, now the Cincinnati Reds, are recognized as the oldest professional baseball franchise in America.

Industrialization and Labor Unrest

As industrialization spread across the country so did labor unrest, and baseball was not immune. Labor unions, in particular the Knights of Labor, which later became the American Federation of Labor (AFL), was formed and grew in strength and numbers. Strikes, along with violence, resonated throughout the country due to poor working conditions and low wages. In baseball, players began questioning their contracts and the reserve clause which in some ways was a paid form of slavery. The first attempt at forming a players union to oppose the reserve clause was in 1885 but it lacked the financial resources to create a serious attack. Some players bolted from their teams and tried to start a Players Association League but it quickly dissolved into bankruptcy and the players were forced to return to the National League and accept the reserve clause if they wished to continue their careers.

Racial Barriers

America and baseball also simultaneously struggled with racial issues. The need for labor in the initial stages of the industrial revolution broke down many racial barriers but as demand evened out and machinery started to take the place of workers, racial barriers began to reappear. The Reconstruction Act of 1867 granting civil rights to Negroes was a failure and was replaced by Jim Crowe laws in the south which mandated segregation of public places. The name Jim Crowe originated from a 1830s dance caricature known as "Jump Jim Crowe" and became a slang synonym for Negro.

Similarly, in the early days of professional baseball, black ballplayers played alongside whites. However beginning in 1887 and lasting until 1946, black ballplayers were excluded from both major and minor league professional baseball, and were forced to form separate leagues. The National Colored Baseball League was formed under the leadership of businessman and entrepreneur Walter Brown. The league was composed of eight teams representing New York, Boston, Philadelphia, Pittsburgh, Cincinnati, Louisville, Baltimore and Washington. In addition to these teams there was already a previously established barnstorming team of popular Negro stars called the Cuban Giants. Baseball mania spread as quickly through the black population as it had the white. Names such as Bud Fowler, Grant "Homerun" Johnson, and Billy Holland became well known. For information regarding Negro League baseball, read *A Game For All Ages* by Henry Metcalf.

The 1887–1888 Cuban Giants. The Giants were the Negro League's first salaried professional baseball team.

There is also a history of baseball being played outside the United States as early as 1872. In Japan it was introduced by an American school teacher and quickly became Japan's most popular sport. From Japan it spread to other Asian countries including China and Korea.

Chinese–American ball club. Baseball in Hawaii quickly explodes in popularity, with organized leagues flourishing by the early 1900s.

The First Hall of Fame Players

In the National League the two biggest stars were Adrian "Cap" Anson and Michael "King" Kelly both of the Chicago White Stockings. "Cap" had a lifetime batting average of .329 and twice batted over .400. He was a feisty little second baseman who played and managed for 22 years. He was considered a model citizen who neither smoked nor drank, which was very much a rarity among the rough farm and factory workers who became major league ball players of this early era. He was inducted into the Hall of Fame in Cooperstown, New York, in 1939. " Cap" was the first professional baseball player to enter politics when, as a Democrat, he was elected as the City Clerk of Chicago in 1906. His political career did not last long. In 1908 he was trounced in an effort to be elected Sheriff after a somewhat scandal-filled term as City Clerk. There have been numerous ball players who turned politician since Cap. The most recent and prominent being Detroit Tiger and Hall of Fame pitcher Jim Bunning, who served as a United States Congressman and Senator from Kentucky 1987-2010.

King Kelly was the first flamboyant star of the game. King was a catcher who could run, hit and slide. He is

Michael "King" Kelly, circa 1887.

Adrian "Cap" Anson, circa 1887.

considered the father of the Chicago Slide, known today as the hook slide. Fans were known to chant "slide Kelly slide" whenever he reached base. He played for 16 years with a lifetime batting average of .308. It was big news when, in 1889, King was sold to the Boston club for an unheard of sum of $10,000. In Boston he was called their "$10,000 Beauty." King is considered baseball's first media darling and became well known, as this was also the birth of modern advertising. He was also the highest paid ballplayer of his time making approximately $5,000 per year. The average player's salary at the time was about $2,000. King was the first ball player to write his autobiography, *Play Ball – Stories of the Ball Field* in 1888. He was inducted into the Hall of Fame in 1941.

A third Hall of Fame member from this early era was Al Spalding— pitcher, manager and president of the Chicago White Stockings. Spalding won 47 of his team's 52 victories in 1876, the first year of organized baseball. As an executive Spalding is given much credit for his management skills in organizing the new league. Following his playing days he became a renown entrepreneur when, in 1876, he with his brothers started a sporting goods store that grew into a chain of outlets stretching from Oregon to Rhode Island. The business sold balls, uniforms, bats and gloves to the new professional league and is still a brand name recognized today.

It is difficult to compare these early statistics with the modern era of baseball primarily due to the change in equipment and rules. The early day players played with, or sometimes without, pancake flat gloves, soft and dirty baseballs and lighter-weight, thinner bats. Home runs were rare, and in the very beginning pitchers threw underhand. The uniforms were baggy, dirty and hot. They looked more like the poor immigrants of the times than the sleekly tailored look of the modern ballplayer. In 1876 Chicago won the pennant with a record of 52 wins and 14 losses, Cap Anson batted .356, the leading home run hitter hit 7 home runs, and the leading runs batted in leader had 60 RBIs. . Although we cannot compare players like Spalding, King and Anson to today's stars such as pitcher Clayton Kershaw of the Los Angeles Dodgers or outfielder Bryce Harper of the Washington Nationals, we do know they were two of the best of their era and deservedly have been included in the National Baseball Hall of Fame in Cooperstown, New York. It would be more than thirty years later before baseball fully standardized its rule and the number of games in a season.

LEFT: Advertisement for AG Spalding and Bros. Athletic Goods (1888), in Harpers Magazine. RIGHT: Albert Goodwill Spalding, as ballplayer for the Boston Red Stockings (1871). Five years later Spalding and his brothers founded the national sporting goods chain which flourishes up to the present day.

LEFT: "Pillow" style catcher's baseball mitt with crescent pad, circa 1897. Source: Keyman Collectibles. RIGHT : The full-fingered "Workman" style baseball glove, circa 1890s.

BELOW: The Spalding line of "Gold Medal Baseball Bats" were made available in the catalogs from 1905–1918. Source: Keyman Collectibles.

Diamonds Shine in the Big Cities

Baseball was following the same path as the USA in its development. Its growing success was largely a result of America's urbanization. The start of the industrial revolution and the large number of immigrants entering the country was creating massive population shifts into the cities. Department stores such as Wanamakers of Philadelphia flourished. The advent of machine tools such as the Singer sewing machine allowed the mass production of readymade fashions. Leisure time activities such as the opening of Coney Island in New York and early film making were creating excitement. Vaudeville shows were the rage for the new society that was seemingly without great class distinction. Factory life was replacing farm life. The man would leave his home in the morning and return in the evening at a set time. Owning a home became the symbol of the American dream.

Between 1885–1890 baseball found its home in the flourishing cities of the Northeast and Midwest. Fans flocked to wooden stadiums that had limited seating capacity but generous standing room. Major League Baseball games attracted over 2 million fans in 1889. Two publications, The Sporting News and Sporting Life, commenced that same year. Ernest Thayer wrote his famous poem *Casey at the Bat*. The rules of the game were evolving close to present day baseball. Teams played 140 games per year and just as today, pitchers threw overhand from 60' 6 " and the bases were 90 feet apart. Bats were standardized and all players wore gloves.

Source: ballparks.com; courtesy of the Franklin Digital Collection.

Baker Bowl, home of the Philadelphia Phillies, which opened on April 30, 1887.

Casey at the Bat

"Casey at the Bat: A Ballad of the Republic Sung in the Year 1888" is a baseball poem written in 1888 by Er-nest Thayer. First published in The San Francisco Examiner (then called The Daily Examiner) on June 3, 1888, it was later popularized by DeWolf Hopper in many vaudeville performances. It has become one of the best-known poems in American literature.

The outlook wasn't brilliant for the Mudville nine that day;
The score stood four to two with but one inning more to play.
And then when Cooney died at first, and Barrows did the same,
A sickly silence fell upon the patrons of the game.

A straggling few got up to go in deep despair. The rest
Clung to that hope which springs eternal in the human breast;
They thought if only Casey could but get a whack at that—
We'd put up even money now with Casey at the bat.

But Flynn preceded Casey, as did also Jimmy Blake,
And the former was a lulu and the latter was a cake;
So upon that stricken multitude grim melancholy sat,
For there seemed but little chance of Casey's getting to the bat.
But Flynn let drive a single, to the wonderment of all,
And Blake, the much despised, tore the cover off the ball;
And when the dust had lifted, and men saw what had occurred,
There was Jimmy safe at second and Flynn a-hugging third.

Then from 5,000 throats and more there rose a lusty yell;
It rumbled through the valley, it rattled in the dell;
It knocked upon the mountain and recoiled upon the flat,
For Casey, mighty Casey, was advancing to the bat.

There was ease in Casey's manner as he stepped into his place;
There was pride in Casey's bearing and a smile on Casey's face.
And when, responding to the cheers, he lightly doffed his hat,
No stranger in the crowd could doubt 'twas Casey at the bat.

Casey at the Bat

Ten thousand eyes were on him as he rubbed his hands with dirt;
  Five thousand tongues applauded when he wiped them on his shirt.
Then while the writhing pitcher ground the ball into his hip,
Defiance gleamed in Casey's eye, a sneer curled Casey's lip.
And now the leather-covered sphere came hurtling through the air,
And Casey stood a-watching it in haughty grandeur there.
Close by the sturdy batsman the ball unheeded sped—
"That ain't my style," said Casey. "Strike one," the umpire said.

From the benches, black with people, there went up a muffled roar,
Like the beating of the storm-waves on a stern and distant shore.
"Kill him! Kill the umpire!" shouted some one on the stand;
And it's likely they'd have killed him had not Casey raised his hand.

With a smile of Christian charity great Casey's visage shone;
He stilled the rising tumult; he bade the game go on;
He signaled to the pitcher, and once more the spheroid flew;
But Casey still ignored it, and the umpire said, "Strike two."

"Fraud!" cried the maddened thousands, and echo answered fraud;
But one scornful look from Casey and the audience was awed.
They saw his face grow stern and cold, they saw his muscles strain,
And they knew that Casey wouldn't let that ball go by again.
The sneer is gone from Casey's lip, his teeth are clinched in hate;

He pounds with cruel violence his bat upon the plate.
And now the pitcher holds the ball, and now he lets it go,
And now the air is shattered by the force of Casey's blow.

Oh, somewhere in this favored land the sun is shining bright;
The band is playing somewhere, and somewhere hearts are light,
And somewhere men are laughing, and somewhere children shout;
But there is no joy in Mudville—mighty Casey has struck out.

Source: Wikimedia Commons.

Illustration from 1912 depicting Casey at the Bat.

Great Americans and News of the Era

1876 Alexander Graham Bell makes first telephone call.

1877 Andrew Carnegie introduces the modern steel industry.

1878 Thomas Edison forms the Edison Light Company.

1878 The Knights of Labor Union was formed. It merged with the American Federation of Labor (AFL) in 1886.

1881 Clara Barton starts the American Red Cross.

1881 Booker T. Washington opens the Tuskegee Institution for Blacks

1882 John L. Sullivan becomes the heavyweight knuckles boxing champion.

1885 George Eastman developed the Kodak box camera.

Famous Authors and Literature of the Era

Louisa May Alcott–*Behind a Mask, Little Men, Under the Lilacs, Little Women*

Mark Twain–*Life on the Mississippi, Adventures of Tom Sawyer*

HG Wells –*The Wonderful Visit, The Time Machine, War of the Worlds*

Walt Whitman–*Song of Myself, Leaves of Grass, November Boughs*

Rudyard Kipling –*The Man Who Would Be King, Gunga Din, The Jungle Book*

Entertainment

Ragtime music– *You've Been a Good Old Wagon But You Done Broke*

Vaudeville stage shows– The development of vaudeville marked the beginning of popular entertainment as big business.

Coney Island opens– Between about 1880 and World War II, Coney Island was the largest amusement area in the United States.

The Greatest Show on Earth–In 1871, the American traveling circus company began its 147-year run.

FROM TOP: Alexander Graham Bell, Thomas Alva Edison, Samuel Clemens (a/k/a "Mark Twain"), John L. Sullivan.

Fashions

Men were called "dude" and dressed classy wearing knickerbockers, Panama hats, monocles, parted their hair down the middle and carried canes. Women wore patent leather shoes with very high heels, floor length skirts, balloon sleeves, small hats with hair pulled back from their forehead and knotted on top with a pompadour.

Baseball Milestones

1876 The National Baseball League is formally organized as an eight team league. Chicago is the champion with 52 wins and 14 losses. Chicago's Al Spalding is the leading pitcher with 42 wins.

1879 The reserve clause restricting each ball player to the services of the owner of that ball club is inserted into all player contracts.

1883 The American Association (AA), later to be the American League, is recognized by the National League (NL) as a minor league association.

1889 Ernest Thayer's poem *Casey at the Bat* is published.

2

A New Century

As They Played The Game

Smokey Joe Wood, pitcher Boston (AL) 1908–1915. Dominant fast ball pitcher until injuries shortened his career.

"I might as well just take a deep breath and come right out and put the matter bluntly: the team I started with was the Bloomer Girls. One day in September this Bloomer Girl team came to Ness City, Kansas. The girls were advertised in posters all around Ness City for weeks before they arrived, you know, and they finally came in town and we played them. Well, after the game the fellow who managed them asked me if I'd like to join and finish the tour with them. There was only three weeks left on the trip, and he offered me $20 if I'd play the infield with them the last three weeks.

(continued on p. 20)

The Gay Nineties was somewhat of a misnomer. The economic prosperity of the country in the 1880s changed dramatically as the new decade arrived. While the country and baseball were still experiencing the initial success from urbanization, there was a lurking recession primarily caused by the trade protection policies of President Grover Cleveland that severely limited imports. Imports were so restricted that American manufacturers took the liberty of raising prices which consequently created tremendous inflation that forced the population to tighten its belt. This, of course, was felt by baseball as attendance dropped. There was also deepening labor problems in the workplace and on the baseball diamond.

As mass production spread to factory floors, employers were following Frederick Taylor's rigid scientific style of management that had little regard for the individual. Industrial jobs were designed for maximum production and woe to the worker who could not keep up with the assembly line. Mass production was spreading to factory floors. The Henry Ford era was on the horizon. The country had gone through a succession of one-term presidents and changing administrations. Neither Presidents Hayes, Garfield, Cleveland nor McKinley were able to demonstrate the leadership needed to ease the country through the industrial transition. The combination of the trade and labor crises caused the "Panic of 1893," an economic depression that lasted for four years.

Baseball players were treated much like the American worker. Their attempt to create a union failed. Owners were victorious

(continued from p. 19) - Smokey Joe Wood

"Are you kidding me,' I asked. "Are you off your rocker?"

"Listen," he said. "You know as well as I do that all those Bloomer Girls are not girls. The third baseman's real name is Bill Compton, not Dolly Madison. And the pitcher, Lady Waddell, sure isn't Rube's sister. If anything he's his brother."

"Well, I figured as much," I said. "But these guys are wearing wigs. If you think I'm going to put a wig on you're crazy."

"No need to," he said. "With your baby face you won't need one anyway."

"Fact is there were four boys on the team: me, Lady Waddell, Dolly Madison, and one other. The other ones were girls. In case you are interested, by the way, the first team, Rogers Hornsby (Hall of Fame third baseman) played on a Bloomer Girls team too. So I am not in such bad company."

Source: The Glory of Their Times

and imposed a $2400 maximum annual player salary. Players of the time were considered a pretty crude and rough group with very little education. They stayed in cheap hotels and worked on farms and in factories during the off season.

Stars of the Era

The 1890s introduced three baseball players that are well known today for their contribution to the history of baseball: Cy Young, Wee Willie Keeler and John McGraw. Boston was the dominant team from '91 through '94 in what had grown to a 12-team league. In 1892 a 154-game schedule was adopted which was followed for the next 65 years. Due to a dwindling of fan interest caused by the competitive imbalance of such a large league the season was split into two halves with the first half winners playing the second half winners for the championship.

LEFT: Denton True "Cy" Young, star pitcher of the 1898 Cleveland Spiders. Source: Baseballhall.org. MIDDLE: John McGraw, manager of the New York Giants (1910). Paul Thompson, photographer. Source: Library of Congress. RIGHT: "Wee Willie" Keeler (circa 1903). Author unknown. Source: Wikimedia Commons.

Boston won the first half as expected but a new team, the Cleveland Spiders, won the second half. The success of this new team was primarily due to a new pitcher – Denton True Young. Young became known as Cy due to his pitches being thrown so hard that they could break through the backstop like a cyclone. Cy was a big farm boy standing 6 feet 2 inches tall and weighed 210 pounds. He went on to pitch 22 seasons, started 906 games and won 510 times – all records that will most likely stand forever. Cy has been immortalized throughout baseball with the annual Cy Young Award given each year to the best pitcher in each league.

1894 brought a new baseball dynasty to the forefront – the Baltimore Orioles. The team was led by by a special player who was destined to create baseball excitement for the next 40 years, initially as a scrawny third baseman with big ears and later as a manager. John McGraw led a band of swashbuckling players who would go to any extreme to win ballgames. They were the first team to perfect the hit and run and squeeze play. They were also known for creative, although not ethical, antics on the field. They would hide a baseball in the deep grass of the outfield so that in the event that they could not get to the one hit, they would pick up the previously hidden ball and throw it into the infield. They were also known to grab the uniforms of runners to slow them down. The win at any cost attitude netted the Orioles three consecutive pennants thanks in large part to adding "Wee Willie" Keeler to the team in 1894. The future Hall of Famer (class of 1939) batted .361 his rookie year and went on to play 19 seasons with a lifetime average of .342. Wee Willie batted .424 in 1897.

America Becomes a World Power

During this time the country was becoming embroiled in the Spanish American War against Spain with the goal of acquiring control of Puerto Rico, Cuba and the Philippine Islands. Future president Teddy Roosevelt was leading the Rough Riders, the first United States Cavalry, in the charge up San Juan Hill. The Rough Riders were a courageous group of volunteers whose fighting power in the Battle of San Juan Hill played a major role in the Spaniards feeing Cuba. By the conclusion of this short war America was being recognized as a world power. In defeating Spain, it colonized Cuba and Puerto Rico and chased the Spaniards out of The Philippines, which lead to securing a military base in the Far East. America had entered the world stage. It spread its influence throughout Central America and the Caribbean. The Panama Canal was built and the country annexed Hawaii, which became an important strategic base. These actions also exposed American baseball to these islands which eventually resulted into the migration of Latino players into the Major Leagues.

The Progressive Era

The beginning of the 20th century marked the start of the Progressive Era. Theodore Roosevelt became President following the assassination of William McKinley in 1901. Roosevelt, although initially seen as a conservative Republican, took aim at corporate abuse. During this time of immense growth and opportunity corporations became very powerful. Power brought corruption and Roosevelt fought against the monopolies and oligopolies that were being created by muscling through the enforcement of the Sherman Antitrust Act which prohibited monopolies.

The Progressive Era also paved the way for the enactment of protective legislation for women, blacks and workers. The women's suffrage movement gained traction and laws were passed to protect women's rights in the workplace. Booker T. Washington became the spokesperson for the

Byron Bancroft "Ban"Johnson, founder and first president of the American League (1921). Johnson developed the American League, a "clean" alternative to the National League, which had become notorious for its rough–and–tumble atmosphere. Source: Library of Congress, Natonal Photo Company Collection.

black population. The NAACP was formed in 1909 as the growing economy opened up jobs for blacks, particularly in the booming industrial Northeast. African-American neighborhoods became an established part of every sizable northern city. Safety regulations were passed partially as a result of a fire at the Triangle Shirtwaist Company in New York City that killed 146 people primarily women and immigrant workers. Upton Sinclair's book, *The Jungle,* addressed the horrible working conditions of the Chicago meatpacking industry and lead to the creation of the Food and Drug Administration. The scientific era of management which was blind to the human needs of workers was being forced to change to a more humanistic approach to workers in many businesses. However the mass production assembly line work at Ford, Bethlehem Steel and many other industrial giants continued to abuse workers with very long hours and monotonous tasks.

Roosevelt was replaced by Republican William Taft in 1908. He did attempt a comeback and nearly succeeded by running for President in 1912 with his personally created, more liberal, "Bull Moose" party. However the result of this third party split the Republican Party and allowed for the election of Democrat Woodrow Wilson in 1912.

In baseball the times were also changing. The undisciplined approach to the game and the greed of the owners eventually led to the creation of a second league, the American League in 1901. Led by Charles

Source: Library of Congress.

President William Howard Taft throws the first pitch of the 1910 season, thus establishing the springtime tradition of ceremonious pitches by U.S. presidents. Source: Library of Congress.

Comiskey, Connie Mack and Ban Johnson they developed a disciplined and highly respected minor league that drew attention away from the National League. Comiskey took Chicago, Mack had Philadelphia and John McGraw deserted the National League to take control of the new American League franchise in Baltimore. Teams were also fielded in Boston, Milwaukee, and Washington. Ban Johnson became president of the new league which became known for its more ethical approach to the game and the fans liked it. The result was a competitive war between the two leagues.

As the march to the cities continued the growing middle class became more entranced with baseball. The creation of the American League added to competition between cities and arguments over the best teams and leagues. The two leagues each had eight teams and played a 154-game schedule which did not include playing any of the other league teams. In 1903 the first official World Series was played between Boston of the American League and Pittsburgh of the National League. The American League defeated the heavily favored National League five games to three in a nine-game series as opposed to the current seven game World Series. The result caused so much embarrassment to the senior league that they refused to play again until 1905. The original teams of the two leagues remained intact until 1957. Attendance grew to over 7 million fans in 1909, the same year that President Taft became the first president to throw out the season's opening pitch. *"Take Me Out to the Ballgame"* became a popular song and new stadiums of concrete and steel began replacing the wooden structures of the 1800s. It was still the dead ball era as the ball had little bounce compared to today's ball. Teams relied on bunting, stealing bases, and squeeze plays and not home runs. Pitchers perfected their craft using spitballs and scuffed baseballs to their advantage. The dominant teams of the early 20th century were the New York Giants and the Chicago Cubs in the National League while Boston, Philadelphia and Detroit fought for supremacy in the American League.

Notable Ballplayers of the Progressive Era

A new cast of characters added to baseball's appeal. Honus Wagner was flourishing in a career that covered fifteen years in which he played in 2785 games and batted .327 while playing shortstop for the Pittsburgh Pirates. He is well known today for the value of his original baseball card that was taken out of print on his declaration that because of his disapproval of smoking, he would not allow his name to be associated with the American Tobacco Company that printed the card. The card sold at auction in 2013 for $2,105,770.50.

Christy Mathewson became a glamour boy pitching for the New York Giants. He was a good looking college educated player who won 373 games including three consecutive years of winning 30 games. In 1905 he pitched in the second World Series and won three games, all shutouts, as the N.Y. Giants won the series four games to one over Connie Mack's Philadelphia Athletics.

Top: The famous T206 Honus Wagner baseball card. On April 6, 2013 it brought in $2,105,770.50 in an online sale by Goldin Auctions.

Right: One of numerous publications (Baseball Magazine, 1914) The Christy Mathewson "The Gentleman's Hurler," has graced during his legendary career. J.F. Kernan, illustrator.

George Edward " Rube" Waddell was a giant for his time. He stood 6 feet 3 inches tall and threw hard. Connie Mack was his manager, which was no easy task as Rube was considered a man-child known for childish behavior; one time he left the pitching mound to chase after a fire engine that was running by the stadium.

Teammate Sam "Wahoo" Crawford had this to say about Waddell:

"Rube" Waddell, pitcher for the St. Louis Browns, with the team mascot (1909). William H. Trefts, Jr., photographer. Source: Missouri History Museum.

You couldn't control him because he was just a big kid. Baseball was just a game to Rube. We'd have a big game scheduled for a Sunday with posters all over town that the great Rube Waddell was going to pitch that day. The little park would be packed, everybody wanted to see Rube pitch but half the time there would be no Rube. The manager would be having a fit. And then just a few minutes before the game there would be a commotion in the grandstand and you'd hear people laughing and yelling "Here comes Rube! Here comes Rube!"

And there he'd come, right through the stands. He'd jump down on to the field, cut across the infield to the clubhouse, taking off his shirt as he went. In about three minutes — he never wore any underwear — he'd run back out in uniform and yell "All right, let's go get 'em !"

The main thing you had to watch out for was not to get him mad. Hughie Jennings, our manager at Detroit, used to go to the dime store and buy little toys like rubber snakes or a jack in the box. He'd get in the first base box and set them in the grass and yell "hey Rube, look" Rube would look over at the jack in the box and kind of grin real slow like you know. Yeah, we'd do anything to get him in a good mood.

Source: Glory of Their Times

Waddell pitched for thirteen seasons, won 191 games and had an incredible lifetime ERA of 2.16. He was elected to the Hall of Fame in 1946.

The Chicago Cubs featured Mordecai "Three Finger " Brown. Mordecai had lost two fingers on his pitching hand in a farm accident. At one time he beat Mathewson nine straight times. "Three Fingers was the ace of a Cubs team that won the World Series four out of five years. That team also featured a well known double-play combination of Tinker (shortstop) to Evers (second base) to Chance (first base).

The Detroit Tigers rose to prominence in the American League largely on the feats of the infamous Ty Cobb. Ty Cobb won the first of his 12 batting titles in 1907. He batted over .400 three times and accumulated 4191 hits, a record that would stand until Pete Rose retired in 1986 with 4256 hits. His statistics include a .367 lifetime batting average, the highest on record, and 829 stolen bases over 24 years. He was known for his tough brand of baseball and using any way possible to score including his cleats up approach to stealing bases. He was the epitome of the tough players of his era. A Georgia boy, he became known as the Georgia Peach. Ty became a successful business man after baseball and made a good-sized fortune from his early purchase of Coca Cola stock.

LEFT: Mordecai Peter "Three Fingers" Brown (1911). Chicago National League. Source: Library of Congress. RIGHT: Tyrus Raymond "Ty" Cobb, of the Detroit Tigers (1913). Published by the National Photo Company. Source: Library of Congress, Prints and Photograph Division.

Fred Merkle (1888-1956)

As They Played The Game

In 1908 there was a play in baseball that became known as the Merkle incident. It was September 23, Giants versus the Cubs, both teams fighting for the pennant. The score was 1-1 in the bottom of the 9th and Giants' Fred Merkle was at bat with a runner on first with one out. Merkle lined a hard single to centerfield with the runner galloping to third. The next batter singled over second base causing the second base umpire to hit the ground to prevent from getting hit. The runner on third scored the winning run and the fans mobbed the field. Meanwhile Merkel, in the excitement took off for the dugout without touching second base. Second baseman Evers asked the outfielder to throw him the ball to touch second base but dropped the relay throw. A Giants player, aware of what Evans was planning, ran out of the dugout, picked up the loose baseball and threw it into the stands. Evans than retrieved a new baseball from the umpire and tagged second base and insisted Merkle be called out claiming he would have been out before the runner scored. Since the second base umpire had ducked, the head umpire ruled for the Cubs and declared the game a tie since the fans had taken over the field. The tie ruling remained since it would not matter unless the season ended with the Giants and the Cubs tied for first, which of course it did. The game was replayed on October 7 to determine the pennant winner. Over 80,000 fans showed up for the game in New York although the stadium could only seat 35,000. Fans were everywhere, on tops of buildings, perched on lamp posts and on each other's shoulders. The pitchers were Christy Mathewson versus "Three Finger" Brown. The Cubs won in a comeback victory and Fred Merkle openly wept due to his error two weeks earlier that mandated playing the game. For many years thereafter when someone would make a mistake it might be referred to as a "Merkle."

Source: Glory of Their Times

Lyrics by Jack Norwath

Katie Casey was baseball mad,
Had the fever and had it bad.
Just to root for the home town crew,
Ev'ry soul
Katie blew.
On a Saturday her young beau
Called to see if she'd like to go
To see a show, but Miss Kate said "No,
I'll tell you what you can do:"

Chorus

Take me out to the ball game,
Take me out with the crowd;
Buy me some peanuts and Cracker Jack,
I don't care if I never get back.
Let me root, root, root for the home team,
If they don't win, it's a shame.

For it's one, two, three strikes, you're out,
At the old ball game.

Katie Casey saw all the games,
Knew the players by their first names.
Told the umpire he was wrong,
All along,
Good and strong.
When the score was just two to two,
Katie Casey knew what to do,
Just to cheer up the boys she knew,
She made the gang sing this song:

Great Americans and News of the Era

1890   Congress passes the Sherman Act outlawing monopolies.

1893   Chicago's World Fair introduces the Ferris wheel.

1896   First modern day Olympic Games commences.

1900   Theodore Roosevelt ascends to the presidency after the
assassination of William McKinley.

1900   Booker T. Washington founded the National Negro Business League.

1901   First radio signal sent to Europe.

1903   Orville and Wilbur Wright fly the first airplane in Kitty Hawk,
North Carolina.

1906   San Francisco earthquake and fire kill over 3000 people and
destroy 80% of the city.

1908   The Ford Model T was introduced to America.

Famous Authors and Literature of the Era

Upton Sinclair—The Jungle, A Prisoner of Morro, The Fasting Cure

Jack London—Call of the Wild, White Fang, The Sea-Wolf, The People
of the Abyss

Stephen Crane—The Red Badge of Courage, War is Kind

Entertainment

Nickelodeons — Usually set up in converted storefronts, these small, simple
theaters, the first tio show projected motion pictures, charged five cents for
admission and flourished from about 1905 to 1915.

John Philip Sousa—Known as "The March King" for his American military
and patriotic marches. Among his best-known marches are The Stars and Stripes
Forever, Semper Fidelis, The Liberty Bell, The Thunderer
and The Washington Post.

Fashions

Women wore large hats with masses of feathers and sometimes stuffed birds.
Skirts rose from floor length to well above the ankles. Men wore sporty
shoes with spats, blazers, knickerbockers and silk top hats.

Baseball Milestones

1901 The American Association of Baseball was organized.

1903 The American Association became the American League of
Major League Baseball.

1903 The Boston Red Stocking defeat Pittsburgh in the
first World Series.

1910 Take Me Out to the Ball Game becomes a popular song.

FROM TOP: Theodore
Roosevelt, Booker T. Washington,
the Wright brothers' first flight at
Kitty Hawk, 1910 Ford Model T,
an 1897 published copy of John
Philip Sousa's Stars & Stripes
Forever, and a poster announcing
the first World Series.

3

A World At Unrest

A feeling of apprehension and unrest gripped the country at the outset of the 1920s. The fragile alliance of European nations was unraveling. Meanwhile there were increasing social tensions between races in the USA spurred primarily by the resurgence of the Klu Klux Klan. The original Klan was organized in 1860 but died out shortly after the Civil War. However, in 1915 William Joseph Simmons of Stone Mountain, Georgia, reorganized the white supremacy hate group. It grew into a powerful and influential group of conservative white Protestants under the premise of protecting America from the danger of African Americans and the immigration of Europeans, primarily Catholics. Its greatest representation was in the Midwest, particularly Indiana, and the southern states. Its membership would grow to 6,000,000 citizens over the next fifteen years before starting to decline.

Emergence of Minority Players

Baseball continued in its segregated tradition. However, it became very aware and threatened by the emergence of the popularity of the Negro Leagues and the excitement generated by their fans. Although some continued to question the ability of the players, exhibition games between the white and black teams proved that the talent was pretty evenly matched. Up to this point black professional baseball was owned and controlled by wealthy white men. That started to change with the emergence of a pitcher, Rube Foster. The 300-pound Foster, along with "Homerun" Johnson, became the first well-known black superstars and drew attention wherever they appeared. Foster's ability and personality provided him with a growing

power base that led him to managing and eventually owning the Chicago Giants, which later became the American Giants. In 1920, largely due to Rube Foster's efforts, the eight-team Negro National League officially commenced and lasted for the next thirty years.

Native Americans were permitted to play in the National League. Hall of Fame pitcher "Chief" Bender, a member of the Ojibwe tribe in Minnesota, played for 16 years, starting in 1903, for Connie Mack's Philadelphia Athletics and enjoyed two seasons as a 20-game winner. The "Chief" was a graduate of the Carlisle (Pa.) Indian Industrial School as was the world famous Olympic athlete and football player Jim Thorpe, who also played briefly for the New York Giants baseball club. John McGraw, manager of the American League Baltimore Orioles, attempted to play Charles Grant, a light-skinned African American second baseman, by passing him off as a Native American named Chief Tokahoma Grant. His ploy was exposed by owner Charles Comiskey of the Chicago White Sox and the prohibition of blacks in the major leagues was upheld.

The Brief Existence of the Federal League

The dominant teams of the second decade of the 20th century were the New York Giants and Philadelphia in the National League while Boston and Philadelphia A's fought for supremacy in the American League. The reserve clause was challenged again in 1914 by an upstart league, the Federal League. The challenging league started play in eight cities and was able to recruit some prominent ball players from the major leagues with promises of large salaries. The major leagues threatened lifetime banishment to any player who dared to switch leagues. The Federal League was short-lived; however, it challenged the legality of the reserve clause and its case ended up in the Supreme Court. Under the leadership of Supreme Court Justice Judge Kenesaw Mountain Landis the court ruled in favor of the Major League Baseball owners by declaring that baseball was a sport and therefore not subject to the laws of industry as applied to monopolies. Judge Landis would later be elected by the owners to be the Commissioner of Major League Baseball. Ironically, during this time, President Roosevelt was fighting against monopolies. It was a monumental ruling that ended the Federal League and remained upheld until challenged in the Supreme Court by St. Louis outfielder Curt Flood in 1969.

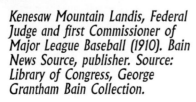

Kenesaw Mountain Landis, Federal Judge and first Commissioner of Major League Baseball (1910). Bain News Source, publisher. Source: Library of Congress, George Grantham Bain Collection.

Stars of the Era

Walter "Big Train" Johnson of the Washington Senators was the era's hardest throwing pitcher. In describing Johnson, Ty Cobb said "You can't hit what you can't see." In one series versus the New York Highlanders (later to be the Yankees) the Train shut them out on Friday, Saturday, and again on Monday. In 21 seasons he set 15 American League records, including 413 wins, 113 shutouts and 5,925 innings pitched. At one time he threw 56 consecutive shutout innings. He was likened to the giant steam locomotives of the era.

Tris Speaker, a fleet-footed centerfielder for the Boston Red Sox, had a lifetime batting average of .345. His fantastic ability with a glove coined the phrase "where triples go to die." In 1917 he batted .386 to win the batting title away from Ty Cobb who had won it for nine consecutive years. He still owns the record for most triples in a career, 200, in addition to setting records in number of assists and double plays by an outfielder. As a player manager for the Cleveland Indians at the end of his career, he was the first to platoon right-handed hitters versus left-handed pitchers and vice versa. Speaker was elected into the Hall of Fame in 1939.

Pitcher Grover Cleveland Alexander of the Philadelphia A's won 28 games in his rookie season, a record that still stands. He won the triple crown of pitching (most wins most strikeouts and lowest era) three times, and threw five no-hitters. In one season he completed 31 games while pitching 367 innings which is more than twice the average for today's Major League pitchers. He was enshrined into the Hall of Fame in 1939, the same year as Tris Speaker.

"Shoeless" Joe Jackson was arguably as fine a hitter as Ty Cobb. The two outfielders competed annually for the batting title. Jackson's career batting average of .356 ranks third all time. He was also acknowledged as a superior outfielder. "Shoeless" gained his nickname due to playing without shoes while in the minor leagues. He played for the Cleveland Naps and the Chicago White Stockings. Due to his involvement with the World Series scandal of 1919 (see end of chapter sidebar) his career ended prematurely.

In addition to Rube Waddell, there was another Rube who stood out during the early 1900s. Rube Marquad (HOF 1971) was a left-handed pitcher for New York and Brooklyn of the National League. He won 211 games and at one time recorded 19 consecutive wins for the Brooklyn Robins, a record that still stands today. During the off season Rube performed as a vaudeville performer. He accompanied actress/singer Blossom Kelly in singing the popular vaudeville song "The Marquard Glide." He later married the glamorous Miss Kelley.

TOP: Walter "Big Train" Johnson (1914). Charles M. Conlon, photographer. Source: Mears Auction.
MIDDLE: Tris Speaker (1912). Bain News Service, author. Source: Library of Congress, Prints and Photographs division. BOTTOM: Grover Cleveland Alexander (1915). Author unknown. Source: Library of Congress, George Grantham Bain Collection

The Black Sox Scandal

**"Shoeless" Joe Jackson
(1887-1951)**

The era ended with a black eye for baseball due to the 1919 World Series scandal. The underdog Cincinnati Reds were taking on the highly favored Chicago White Sox. The Sox had it all — great pitching, and great hitting, led by the incomparable "Shoeless Joe Jackson." Joe and seven other players, who despised the misery of owner Charles Comiskey, agreed to fix the series with a known gambler, Arnold Rothstein. Although the deal became unhinged halfway through the series, the damage done in the early games allowed the Reds to upset the Sox. The eight players went on trial in 1920 and although acquitted in court due to lack of evidence, they were banned from baseball for life by then

(continued on p. 33)

World War I

In 1917 America joined forces with the Allied Powers of Great Britain, France, and Russia against the Centrist powers of Germany, Austria-Hungary and Turkey. The war broke out in 1915 when the Germans sunk the British cruise liner, The Lusitania, killing 1,198 passengers and crew members. During the next three years the war spread into the Middle East, Africa and China. It became known as the Great War. The USA under the leadership of President Woodrow Wilson held onto its original neutral position until Germany, believing that the American cargo ships were carrying weapons and supplies to the Allied Powers, used submarines, known as U Boats, to attack them without warning. In May of 1918 American troops joined France and Allied Forces outside of Paris to force the Germans into a full retreat by September of the same year. WWI saw the introduction of air warfare. American Eddie Rickenbacker became famous for his flying victories and received the Congressional Medal of Honor. Americans also heard a lot about a German flying hero known as "The Red Baron" who shot down over 80 enemy aircraft. Today's generations know the Red Baron from his cartoon encounters in Charles Schultz's beloved comic strip "Peanuts." On the ground Sergeant Alvin York was regarded as a hero for his ferocious ground combat role against the Germans. He also received the Medal of Honor.

Over a million US troops helped break the German defense and brought the war to an end. The Treaty of Versailles to end the war was signed on June 28, 1919. The total US involvement was over two million troops, with 53,000 dead and 213,000 wounded. Overall, eight million troops from both sides lost their lives.

Baseball was not spared from the war. Most minor league teams suspended operations and the major leagues shortened their seasons in 1917 from 154

Lieutenant Christy Mathewson and Captain Ty Cobb (1918).

> ### (continued from p. 32) - The Black Sox Scandal
>
> Commissioner Kenesaw Mountain Landis. "Shoeless" claimed that he did not go along with the ploy, which was backed by his batting .375 in the World Series with no errors. The media had a frenzy with the story. The statement, "Say it ain't so Joe," supposedly from a 12-year-old fan of Jackson, epitomized the fans' agony and disappointment. The story has become baseball legend. The book, "Eight Men Out," in 2005 became a hit movie, and "Shoeless Joe" was a featured character in the award-winning movie *Field of Dreams* in 1989.

games to 140 in order for players to report to duty before Labor Day. 772 professional baseball players served in the armed forces, as many as 15 players from a particular team. Eight Major League and eight Negro League players sacrificed their lives in the war effort. Many notable Hall of Fame players served in the armed forces. These included Christy Mathewson, Ty Cobb, Grover Cleveland Alexander, Casey Stengel and Tris Speaker. Mathewson was never able to return to his prewar dominance after becoming a victim of a gas attack when training for combat against the Germans.

Spring Training

Beginning in 1886 teams played an abbreviated spring training in Hot Springs, Arkansas. Because of the healing associated with natural warm mineral springs, Hot Springs had become a popular destination for tourists. Also those afflicted by various disabilities caused primarily by arthritis and other joint related ailments found relief in the springs. In 1886 Al Spalding, president of the Chicago White Stockings, gathered his team together in Hot Springs to practice and benefit from the springs. By 1894 they were joined by the majority of teams which created an additional tourist audience in the town. The influx brought new hotels, casinos, horse racing and night time entertainment to the city, creating a Las Vegas environment. The hard drinking, fun-loving players of the era loved to come to spring training. Starting in 1920 many of the Negro League teams joined in the fun. Most of the great ball players from the first half of the twentieth century began their careers in Hot Springs. A young unknown, Babe Ruth, was one of them. In 1918 as a pitcher

1912 Boston Red Sox, Oaklawn Park, Hot Springs, Arkansas

for the Red Sox he began to show his hitting prowess by hitting two homeruns in his first game strictly as a hitter — one of them measured 573 feet. Hot Springs, Arkansas, is considered the birthplace of spring training. A 2015 documentary film, *The First Boys of Spring*, has been shown repeatedly on PBS.

The baseball heyday for Hot Springs lasted into the 1940s. By then Major League teams seeking warmer weather established individual training sites in Florida. For a few years the Dodgers and Yankees also set up camps in Cuba and the Dominican Republic. The Florida training sites became known as the Grapefruit League. There are two popular myths associated with the naming of the Grapefruit League. One involves Casey Stengel, manager of the Yankees, who reportedly threw a grapefruit at Dodger manager Wilbert Robinson. The other myth stemmed from an arranged prank by aviator Ruth Law to drop a baseball from her plane for manager Robinson to catch. The plan was disrupted when Law forgot the baseball and replaced it with a grapefruit that exploded on the face of Robinson upon impact.

In 1947, owner of the Cleveland Indians, Bill Veeck, moved the team's spring training site to Tucson, partly because of southern racism. That was the year that Cleveland signed Larry Doby, the first African American, to play in the American League. The Indians were joined that year by the New York Giants and by the 1950s, six other teams. That was the start of what is now the Cactus League, which consists of 15 teams which train in Arizona.

A Superstar is Born

The Black Box scandal of 1919 left a bitter taste in the mouths of baseball fans. However, it did not last long due to the growing popularity and personality of a very special young ballplayer: George Herman Ruth, better known as "Babe" Ruth. As America entered the Roaring Twenties the country and professional baseball opened its hearts to this exciting orphaned ballplayer from Baltimore.

> "I still can't believe what I saw. This nineteen-year-old kid, crude, poorly educated, only lightly brushed by the social veneer we call civilization, gradually transformed into the idol of American youth and the symbol of baseball the world over – a man loved by more people and with an intensity of feeling that perhaps has never been equaled before or since. I saw a man transformed from a human into something pretty close to a god.
>
> You probably remember him with that big belly he got later on. But that wasn't there in 1914. George was six foot two and weighed 198 pounds, all of it muscle. He had a slim waist, huge biceps, no self- discipline, and not much education – not so different from a lot of other nineteen-year-old would be ball players. Except for two things, he could eat more than anyone else, and he could hit a baseball further."
>
> — Harry Hooper, outfielder, Boston Red Sox
> 1909-1924
> (*The Glory of Their Times*)

Let's Play Baseball Trivia

Trivia Challenge # 1 – 1876 to 1920

Baseball fans love to play baseball trivia. It has been going on since 1876. This will be the first of four quizzes to sharpen your trivia skills.

1. The $10,000 Beauty was the nickname given to:
a. Cap Anson
b. King Kelly
c. John McGraw
d. Al Spalding

2. Who won 47 of his team's 52 victories?
a. Grant Johnson
b. Al Spalding
c. Cap Anson
d. King Kelly

3. Which team is the oldest professional baseball franchise in the USA?
a. Boston Red Stockings
b. Philadelphia Athletics
c. New York Giants
d. Cincinnati Red Stockings

4. Name the Hall of Fame player who played for the Bloomer Girls?
a. Rogers Hornsby
b. Cy Young
c. Smokey Joe Wood
d. Cap Anson

5. Cy Young won
a. 230 games
b. 480 games
c. 305 games
d. 510 games

6. The first President to throw out the first pitch of the season was
a. William McKinley
b. William Howard Taft
c. Teddy Roosevelt
d. Woodrow Wilson

Trivia Challenge # 1 – 1876 to 1920

7. The first World Series was played in
a. 1903
b. 1910
c. 1920
d. 1876

8. Ty Cobb still holds the record for
a. Highest career batting average
b. Most career hits
c. Most hits in a season
d. Most stolen bases

9. Walter "Big Train" Johnson pitched for
a. Detroit Tigers
b. Washington Senators
c. Philadelphia A's
d. Boston Red Sox

10. Which Hall of Fame pitcher was a victim of a gas attack in World War 1?
a. Grover Cleveland Alexander
b. Satchel Paige
c. Christy Mathewson
d. Walter Johnson

11. "Shoeless" Joe was an outfielder for
a. White Sox
b. Reds
c. Yankees
d. Pirates

12. Which African American ball player was most influential in organizing the National Negro League?
a. Grant Johnson
b. Charles Grant
c. Rube Foster
d. Satchel Paige

Answers: 1. b 2. b 3. d 4. a 5. d 6. b 7.a 8. a 9. b 10. c 11. a 12. c

Great Americans and News of the Era

1912 Woodrow Wilson elected President defeating Teddy Roosevelt and William Taft.

1913 The Federal Reserve Bank is formed.

1915 British cruise line ship the Lusitania is sunk by a German U boat, killing

1198 crew and passengers including 128 Americans. War in Europe erupts.

1917 United States enters the war.

1918 Armistice Day— World War I, "The war to end all wars," concludes.

1918 Worldwide flu epidemic killing 23 million, including 550,000 Americans.

1919 President Woodrow Wilson proposes The League of Nations.

Famous authors and Literature of the Era

Edith Wharton – Ethan Frome, Tales of Men and Ghosts,
    The Custom of the Country

Robert Frost – The Road Not Taken, Choose Something Like a Star,
    Mending Wall

T.S. Elliott – Portrait of a Lady, Morning at the Window, Whispers of
        Immortality

Sinclair Lewis – Free Air, The Trail of the Hawk,
                The Innocents: A Story for Lovers

Entertainment

Silent Movies – Birth of a Nation, Intolerance, Broken Blossoms,
 Way Down East

Stars of the Silver Screen– Charlie Chaplain. Douglas Fairbanks, Gloria
 Swanson, Mary Pickford, Lilian Gish

Popular Tunes – Joplin began publishing music in 1895. Some of his best-
    known works include The Entertainer, March Majestic, and
    the short theatrical work The Ragtime Dance.

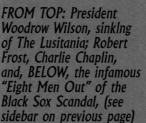

FROM TOP: President Woodrow Wilson, sinklng of The Lusitania; Robert Frost, Charlie Chaplin, and, BELOW, the infamous "Eight Men Out" of the Black Sox Scandal, (see sidebar on previous page)

Fashions

During World War I women took on jobs formerly filled by men.
As they dressed for new roles, gender-dictated dress codes relaxed.
Skirts became shorter, and colors became sober and muted.

Baseball Milestones

1914 The Federal League challenges the NL and AL in the courtroom and
    loses.

1914 Weeghman Park (later renamed Wrigley Field) opens as home for the
    Federal league's Chicago Whalers.

1919 Cincinnati defeats Chicago White Sox in the 1919 World Series
    leading to the Black Sox Scandal (see sidebar on previous page).

4

The Roaring Twenties and the Great Depression

The "Roaring Twenties" arrived full of hope and prosperity, ushering in the beginning of the modern era. It was a time of celebration – peace, new fashions, the Charleston, women's right to vote, talking movies, speakeasies, F. Scott Fitzgerald, and in baseball, Babe Ruth. Life in America was exciting.

Baseball was moving into the Babe era. Ty Cobb and Rogers Hornsby were joined by Babe Ruth in what became the end of the dead ball era. The Babe, who was discovered playing baseball for an orphanage in Baltimore, Md., blossomed into a star pitcher who could also hit homeruns for the Boston Red Sox. In 1920 in what turned out to be the biggest bargain in the history of baseball, the New York Yankees bought the Babe from the Red Sox for $100,000. Ruth had been originally signed as a pitcher with the Sox and he was a darn good one having won 94 games, including 23 in 1916 and 24 in 1917 with a career earned run average of 2.28. But the Yankees were not interested in him as a pitcher because they had witnessed the destruction he could do as a part time hitter. The Babe became a right fielder who could play every day and swing his ferocious bat 600 times per year. In his first year with the Yanks he hit 54 homeruns, 27 more than any other player had accumulated in the history of the game. Babe also batted .378 that season with 14 stolen bases.

As They Saw The Game

Pat Pieper, The Cubs' legendary PA announcer, once told the Chicago Tribune's David Condon:

"Don't let anyone tell you that Babe Ruth didn't call that shot. I was in a perfect position to see and hear everything.

With two strikes, Ruth lifted his bat, pointed toward the center field flag pole, and dug in for Charlie Root's next pitch. That was the most terrific homerun I've ever seen. It went out of the park at almost precisely the same spot that Ruth had indicated. As far as I'm concerned that ball is still traveling. You bet your life Babe Ruth called it."

One thing is for sure: Something of considerable magnitude occurred during the fifth inning of Game 3 of the series. Ruth was being taunted by Cubs players who were actually standing on the field. The crowd was in a frenzy, as the Cubs finally seized momentum to tie the game at 4-4. Ruth responded vehemently with not one but several dramatic gestures, suggesting he was going to do something bad to the Cubs. Then he hit one of the longest homers in Wrigley Field history, which effectively sealed the World Series for the Yankees.

*Ed Sherman
from his book: Babe Ruth's Called Shot*

As They Saw The Game

The death of Cleveland Indians batter Ray Chapman, from a pitch thrown by New York Yankees pitcher Carl Mays in 1920, led to the enactment of a new safety rule: pitchers were barred from throwing the popular spitball. Stanley Covelski, Cleveland Indians pitcher (1916–1928), described his spitball as follows:

"The pitch, the spitball, kept me up there (major leagues) for thirteen years and won me over 200 games.. I got so I had as good of control over the spitball as I did my other pitches. I could make it break any of three ways: down, out, or down and out. And I always knew which way it would break. Depended on my wrist action. For the spitball, what you do is wet these first two fingers. I used alum, had it in my mouth. Sometimes it would pucker your mouth some, get gummy. Sometimes I'd go maybe two or three innings without throwing one. But I'd always have them looking for it. They outlawed the pitch in December of 1920. They wanted to shift the odds more in favor of the batter." [Glory of Their Times]

Although outlawed, pitchers have found clever ways to wet their fingers in various ways ever since. Umpires are often asked by the opposing manager to check to see if the pitcher is cheating. Hall of Fame pitcher Gaylord Perry, 1962-1983, won 314 games, relying on his not so secret pitch, the spitball.

Ruth became the greatest home run hitter of all time until Henry Aaron of the Atlanta Braves hit #715 on April 8, 1974. In addition to hitting home runs at a pace that was inconceivable at the time, Babe's magnetic personality won the hearts of America. He was fun, generous and the idol of men, women and children. Ruth's celebrity led to the opening of Yankee Stadium, "The House That Ruth Built," in 1923. It was considered an architectural marvel.

The National Pastime

The emergence of Ruth, Lou Gehrig and the Yankees could not have come at a better time as the country was welcoming mass communication through movies, magazines and the radio. There was no NFL or NBA. Baseball held center stage. Radio announcers could not get enough of Ruth and Gehrig of the Yanks, Ty Cobb of the Tigers and Rogers Hornsby, the infielder for the St. Louis Cardinals of the National League, who batted over .400 three times. This truly was when baseball became the national pastime The Yankees became the powerhouse of baseball.

The old Polo Grounds in New York drew in crowds to watch the New York Yankees, New York Giants and New York Mets as the game of baseball became the nation's pastime.

Source: ballparksofbaseball.com

In 1927 Ruth hit a record-setting 60 homeruns and along with the "Iron Horse" Lou Gehrig, led the 1927 Yanks in winning 110 games while losing only 44 and swept Pittsburgh 4 games to 0 in the World Series. That championship team is considered by many as the greatest team of all time. The "Iron Horse" went on to play in 2,130 consecutive games, a record that stood for over 60 years until Cal Ripken broke it in 1995. Gehrig compiled a lifetime batting average of .340 with 493 homeruns over 17 seasons. Often overshadowed by teammate Ruth, he was in many ways his equal. He particularly stood out in World Series play in which he batted .361 in seven World Series. Tragically he was forced to retire in 1939 after being diagnosed with ALS, now commonly referred to as Lou Gehrig's disease.

(From left) Lou Gehrig, Tris Speaker, Ty Cobb, and Babe Ruth (1928).
Source: International Newsreel.

The Roaring Twenties

Warren J. Harding was seated in the White House at the beginning of the decade and the economy was growing at a record pace. Stock market investors evidently thought the bull market would never end. The automotive industry was leading the way. Henry Ford's Model T was dominant but new entrants into the automobile market included Chevrolet, Dodge, and Chrysler. Mass production was evident in factories throughout the country. Making newspaper headlines in the early twenties were: the Scopes Trial, which drew national attention to the question of whether evolution should be taught in public schools; President Harding's sudden death, and the Teapot Dome Scandal that exposed bribery when President Harding's Secretary of the Interior was found guilty of accepting bribes from the Teapot Dome Oil Company of Wyoming.

The Women's Suffrage Movement gained the women's right to vote with the passage of the 19th Amendment in 1920. In the same year the Women's Christian Temperance Union achieved its objective with the passing of the Prohibition Act, outlawing liquor. Of course that did not slow down the creative Americans of the time as speakeasy bars opened and prospered throughout the country. Prohibition was a boon for whiskey bootleggers and organized crime. Notorious gangsters made fortunes smuggling liquor and operating illegal clubs. Al Capone became famous in Chicago for his gangster activities including the Valentine Massacre of 1927 in which seven opposing gang members were gunned down by his henchmen. Other famous criminals of the time included

Bonnie and Clyde, John Dillinger, Pretty Boy Floyd and Baby Face Nelson.

In 1927 Ruth and the Yankees had to share the spotlight with Charles Lindbergh, the pioneer aviator who in his plane, The Spirit of St. Louis, was the first to fly across the Atlantic. Lindbergh was a hero in the USA and Europe. Everywhere he went crowds gathered and parades were held in his honor. He was the Neil Armstrong of the era. However his life took a tragic turn on March 1, 1932 when his 20-month old son, Charles Augustus Lindbergh Jr., was kidnapped from home in Hopewell, N.J. The kidnapper demanded $50,000 which was paid but the child was never returned. The boy's body was discovered May 12 having been killed by a blunt force to the head. Bruno Hauptman was arrested, convicted and electrocuted for the murder on April 3, 1936. It was one of the biggest news stories of the 1930s.

Left: A collage, including Charles Lindbergh's portrait from a U.S. postage stamp, marks Lindbergh's historic flight across the Atlantic in 1927.

Bottom: Copies of news clippings from the era provide news on the "daring flier."

The Great Depression

The country was shocked when the stock market crashed in 1929. The Depression that followed brought ten years of a failing economy. Herbert Hoover was in the White House and was unable to turn the tide. Unemployment rose to a staggering 25% by 1933. Food lines became a common sight in most communities. Franklin Roosevelt was elected as the 32nd President in 1932 with the hope of pulling the country out of this spiral.

Major League Baseball was not spared from The Depression. Attendance dropped as did players' salaries. The average player salary of $6,000 went unchanged for over a decade.

Fortunately owners started receiving advertising revenues from the radio networks.

The Negro Leagues proved their resilience as their exposure grew by playing well in exhibition games against Major League All Stars, including a team led by Ruth. Future Hall of Famer "Cool Papa" Bell made his debut as an outfielder in 1922 with the St. Louis Stars of the Negro League. "Cool Papa" was one of the first Negro League All Stars inducted into the National Baseball Hall of Fame in 1974.

LEFT:
James "Cool Papa" Bell.

RIGHT: Leroy Satchel Paige.

Photos courtesy of the Negro League Baseball eMuseum.

Possibly the greatest highlight of the Negro Leagues was the appearance of a young pitcher, Leroy Satchel Paige, in 1926. Satchel was the ultimate showman of the Negro Leagues and eventually the major leagues when he was finally allowed to join the Cleveland Browns in 1948 at the age of 42. Although he was primarily associated with the Kansas City Monarchs, Paige jumped from team to team in the Negro Leagues to whomever held out the most money. He became a household name as he roamed the country on barnstorming teams during the off seasons. He would pitch over a hundred games a year. A popular movie, *The Bingo Long Traveling All Stars & Motor Kings* in 1976, depicts the lifestyle that Satchel and his teammates on the Indianapolis Clowns enjoyed during this era. The Clowns were a baseball team that performed in an entertaining manner similar to the Harlem Globetrotters Basketball Team. Satchel was so confident of his fast ball that at times he would call his outfielders in and tell them to sit down as he struck out the next batter. He once struck out 21 batters in an exhibition game versus Major League All Stars. He continued barnstorming during off seasons and after his Major League career ended in 1953. He resurfaced for one game in 1965 with the Kansas City Athletics of the American League at the age of 59. Satchel was inducted into the Hall of Fame in 1971.

The New Deal

It did not happen overnight but the creation of Roosevelt's New Deal in 1933 started a slow turn around. Welfare programs were started to help the homeless and unemployed. Social security was enacted in 1935 to aid the elderly. The Civil Conservation Corp was formed to put many Americans back to work building national and state parks and other major government projects. Adding to the misery of the country was a tremendous drought in the Midwest and in particular Oklahoma. The drought area became known as the Dust Bowl. Author John Steinbeck's famous novel *The Grapes of Wrath* illustrated the pain of those who suffered through the drought.

Depression-era Heroes

As the country struggled with its emergence from The Great Depression a host of new star players appeared in the major leagues. Ball park revenues increased with the selling of beer following the end of prohibition. The first nighttime game was played in 1935 in Cincinnati. The Yankees continued their dominance of the American League while the Giants, Cubs and Cardinals dominated the National League. Three future Hall of Famers were setting records. Jimmy Foxx and Lefty Grove were playing for Connie Mack's Philadelphia A's of the American League. Foxx, a first baseman, hit 534 homeruns while playing primarily for the A's and Red Sox, while Lefty Grove recorded 300 wins. Outfielder Mel Ott of the New York Giants was beginning his record of leading his team in homeruns for 18 consecutive years. A record that may never be broken. The 1934 World Series champion St. Louis Cardinals were nicknamed the " Gashouse Gang" due to their shabby appearance and supposedly their bad body odor. They were led by pitchers "Dizzy" Dean, a 30-game winner that year, and his brother " Daffy," a 19-game winner. Feisty shortstop Leo Durocher was the captain of this colorful team. Durocher went on to become a Hall of Fame manager.

The Depression was over and things were looking good but similar to twenty years earlier, there were anxieties arising from stories coming out of Europe.

TOP LEFT: Mel Ott (1940) Author: Play Ball Cards, Published by Bowman Gum. TOP MIDDLE; Jay Hannah "Dizzy" Dean (1940). Featured on the April 4, 1935 cover of Time magazine. Credit: Acme Newspictures. TOP RIGHT: Paul Dee "Daffy" Dean (1940). Author: Play Ball Cards, Published by Bowman Gum.

The 1937 All–Stars (July 7, 1937). (From left) Lou Gehrig, Joe Cronin, Bill Dickey, Joe DiMaggio, Charlie Gelringer, Jimmie Foxx, and Hank Greenberg. All seven have been inducted into Baseball's Hall of Fame. Author: Harris & Ewing Source: Library of Congress, Prints and Photographs division.

"It's funny what a few no hitters do for a body."

Satchel Paige, the Hall of Fame pitcher of the Negro Leagues and Major Leagues from the 1920s until 1965, was also known for his wit and practical advice and quotes.

"How old would you be if your didn't know how old you are?"

"Ain't no man can avoid being born average, but there ain't no man got to be common."

"Don't look back. Something might be gaining on you."

Don't look back. Something might be gaining on you.

Satchel Paige

www.thequotes.in

"Just take the ball and throw it where you want it. Throw strikes. Home plate don't move."

"Work like you don't need the money. Love like you have never been hurt. Dance like nobody's looking."

"Sometimes I sits and thinks, and sometimes I just sits."

"Age is a question of mind over matter. If you don't mind, it doesn't matter."

"Airplanes may kill you, but they ain't likely to hurt you."

"Don't pray when it rains if you don't pray when the sun shines."

"The only change is that baseball has turned Paige from a second class citizen to a second class immortal."

"If your stomach disputes you, lie down and pacify it with good thoughts."

Money and women. They're two of the strongest things in the world. The things you do for a woman you wouldn't do for anything else. Same with money."

"I never had a job. I just always played baseball."

Great Americans and News of the Era

1921 Warren J Harding becomes President

1923 President Harding dies.

1924 Calvin Coolidge elected President.

1928 Herbert Hoover elected President.

1929 The stock market crashes. The St. Valentine Massacre headlines the news.

1930 Gangster Al Capone is convicted of tax evasion.

1932 Franklin Roosevelt elected President.

1933 The New Deal commences. Adolph Hitler elected Chancellor of Germany.

1935 Social Security enacted. The Dust Bowl in the Midwest hits its peak

Literature and Entertainment

1920s The Charleston becomes the dancing rage

1925 Scott Fitzgerald writes The Great Gatsby.

1926 Ernest Hemingway publishes his first novel, The Sun Also Rises.

1927 The Jazz Singer becomes first movie with sound.

Baseball Milestones

1923 Yankee Stadium opens

1927 Babe Ruth hits 60 homeruns

1935 First Major League night game in Cincinnati

1935 Babe Ruth retires

FROM TOP: Presidents Herbert Hoover and Franklin D. Roosevelt, Ernest Hemingway, poster for The Jazz Singer.

LEFT: Opening Day at Yankee Stadium, featuring the "March King" John Philip Sousa (second from right).

5

World War II

The world moved closer to World War II when newspapers reported that Germany invaded Poland in 1939. Americans, being comforted by President Franklin Roosevelt's weekly radio broadcasts, went on with life as usual. They escaped their anxieties by turning to sports. Jack Dempsey was the heavyweight champion boxer, Red Grange "The Galloping Ghost" was running the football at Ohio State, and the Four Horsemen were leading Notre Dame. Bobby Jones was popularizing golf and Sea Biscuit was winning horse races. In music, it was the jazz age. The movie *Gone With the Wind* premiered in Atlanta in 1939. Orson Welles frightened many Americans who believed his radio broadcast of *The War of the Worlds*, a dramatic story of the invasion of aliens, was for real. Authors Ernest Hemingway and John Steinbeck entertained the reading public with their bestselling novels.

DiMaggio and Williams

In baseball, the stage was being set for a duel between outfielders Joe DiMaggio of the Yankees and Ted Williams of the Red Sox for hitting supremacy. Throughout the 1940s these two outfielders battled for the American League batting championship. In 1941 Williams batted .407 and became the last player to reach the .400 mark. On the last day of the season, when asked if he would prefer to sit out the doubleheader and protect his .400 average, Williams refused. He played in both games, collected 5 hits to finish at .407. One time when asked what he wished to have engraved on his tombstone, he responded, "The greatest hitter that ever lived." He retired with a .344 batting average, 521 homeruns and 2018 runs batted in. These numbers would have been greatly enhanced if not for having his career interrupted by serving three years as a

As They Saw The Game (continued from page 37)

chosen to accompany American All Stars on a trip to Japan. Many wondered why a part-time weak hitting catcher was chosen to play with a team that featured such stars as Babe Ruth. During the trip Moe would often slip way with his camera to take movies of Japanese buildings including munitions facilities.

In 1942, following his baseball career, Moe was officially recruited into the CIA, who used his movies in planning bombing raids against Japan. It is also known that during the war Moe spent time in Germany where he was assigned to help unveil German atomic capabilities. He was part of a team organized to assassinate the German director of the Nazi Atom Bomb Research Program. The attempted plot was called off at the last minute. He stayed with the CIA for 10 years. Little is known about other roles that Moe played. He died in 1972 before writing his memoir, in which he had pledged to tell the whole story.

pilot in both WWII and Korean War.

That same year DiMaggio hit in 56 consecutive games, a record that still stands. Many are not aware that after not recording a hit in game 57, DiMaggio went on to gather hits in the next 37 consecutive games. DiMaggio beat out Williams for the Most Valuable Player award that season, a decision that haunted Williams for the rest of his life. "Joltin Joe" went on to lead the Yankees to 10 World Series Championships while batting .325, with 361 homeruns and 1,537 runs batted in while also missing three years to active military service. DiMaggio is also remembered for his Hollywood marriage to movie star Marilyn Monroe after his retirement.

Left: Autographed Ted Williams baseball card as part of the All-Time All-Stars collection. Right: A Joe DiMaggio card highlights "The Streak" in which DiMaggio hit .408 during a record-holding 56-game streak in 1941, the longest in Major League baseball history. Images courtesy of Baseball Almanac.

As They Played The Game

ROSEN   *GREENBERG*

Hank Greenberg (HOF), primarily a first baseman of Detroit Tigers (1930-1947), and third baseman Al Rosen (Cleveland Indians 1947-1956) were both known as "The Hebrew Hammer." Greenberg was the first Jewish superstar in American team sports. Known for his prodigious power, the five-time all star led the AL in homeruns and RBIs four times including hitting 58 homeruns in 1938. He had a lifetime batting average of .313. Greenberg served 47 months in the military during WWII, the longest of any ball player.

Al Rosen, also a WWII veteran, inherited the nickname in 1947. In 1953 he was named the American League MVP and barely missed winning the triple crown.

(continued to page 50)

America Enters the War

While war raged throughout Europe in 1940 and 1941, the USA tried to not get involved by declaring itself neutral. However President Roosevelt and Congress did offer support to Great Britain by supplying arms and war materials, but no troops were engaged. The neutrality ended on December 7, 1941, when the Japanese bombed Pearl Harbor, killing more than 2400 Americans and destroying critical elements of our Navy. The attack united Americans, similar to the effect of September 11, 2001. President Roosevelt declared war on Japan the following day in a speech declaring December 7 as "a date which will live in infamy." Three days later, Hitler and Nazi Germany declared war on America and America responded in kind. The war was fought across six continents and accounted for 50 million deaths and hundreds of millions wounded in mind and body. The war in Europe ended in 1945 following the successful Normandy invasion in 1944. Later in 1945 the United States dropped two atomic bombs on the Japanese cities of Hiroshima and Nagasaki forcing the surrender of Japan. Shortly afterward President Truman signed the Marshall Plan which provided support to the rebuilding of Europe, including Germany.

The war impacted our entire society in politics, economics, family life, and of course, baseball and leisure activities. Everything seemed to be put on hold. Families had to undergo significant changes in their lifestyle. Millions of families sent their sons and daughters into the armed forces. Women substituted for the men in defense factories. All Americans were forced to change their buying habits as Congress passed legislation limiting the amount of certain goods such as fuel oil, rubber, meat, butter and sugar that could be purchased due to war shortages. To counter the shortage of fuel oil, schools and restaurants shortened their hours and homeowners were told to lower their heat registers to 65 degrees. Drivers were not allowed to drive more than 35 miles per hour. Manufacturers of automobiles, radios and appliances were forced to switch to military production. Consumer goods were rationed and families received ration books to control their purchases including certain food items.

In an effort to keep baseball in the public's eye, chewing gum mogul Phillip Wrigley started The All American Girls Professional Baseball League in 1943. Based primarily in midwestern cities, the league operated through 1953 attracting over 900,000 attendees and 600 players. Once firmly established the teams played 110 games per season. In its peak season, 1945,

As They Played The Game (continued from page 49)

That year he batted .336 with 43 homeruns and 145 RBIs.

Following his injury shortened career, Rosen became a distinguished baseball executive. He was featured, along with Greenberg and Sandy Koufax, in the 2010 movie, *Jews in Baseball: An American Love Story*. They also shared the distinction of being Jewish and enduring anti–Semitic slurs by players and fans throughout their careers. Both stood strong in defense of their religion. There were many fans who resented their refusal to play games on Jewish holidays Yom Kippur and Rosh Hoshanah. The poet Edgar Guest wrote regarding Greenberg's decision to sit out Yon Kippur, "We shall miss him on the infield and shall miss him at bat/but he is true to his religion and I honor him for that."

Greenberg said, " I wanted to be remembered not only as a great ballplayer, but even more as a great Jewish ballplayer. Rosen, an amateur boxer, sometimes reacted angrily to the slurs: "There's a time that you let it be known that enough is enough ... You flatten them." Both players are in the International Jewish Hall of Fame.

the Rockford Peaches beat the Fort Wayne Chicks in the championship series. Rockford pitcher Carolyn Morris won 28 games that year including a perfect game. The fictionalized story of the league can be seen in the movie, A League of Their Own, starring Tom Hanks. In addition to the women's league, barnstorming teams such as The House of David (below right) entertained baseball fans during the war years.

LEFT: *All American Girls Professional League members performing calisthenics, Opalocka, FL (1948). Source: Florida Memory. The clubs represented are, from left, Fort Wayne Daisies, Chicago Colleens, Rockford Peaches, South Bend Blue Sox, Springfiels Sallies, and Peoria Redwings.* **RIGHT:** *Members of The House of David team from Benton Harbor, Michigan. The Adventist Cult team originated in the 1920s and grew to three barnstorming squads by the 1940s. They played over 200 games per season, usually with a winning percentage of over .700. They were one of the first organized white teams to play against the Negro League teams which helped pave the way to baseball's integration.*

Opportunity and Denial

The demand for labor during the war allowed opportunities for black Americans, which resulted in a large migration of more than one million African Americans from the South to the more industrialized North. However racial discrimination continued, including in the military where the vast majority of the approximately 700,000 black soldiers were assigned menial jobs. The Tuskegee Airmen, a unit of 996 pilots and 15,000 ground personnel, were the first black military aviators to serve and showed the value of the black servicemen. They were credited with 15,500 combat sorties and earned over 150 Distinguished Flying Crosses.

Jews also felt the pains of discrimination in the USA with some organizations declaring them as not eligible for membership. In June of 1941 President Roosevelt issued an executive order which prohibited " discrimination of workers in defense industries, or government, because of race, creed or national origin." This action was unprecedented and was the first in a wave of the many equal opportunity acts to come.

Ironically at the same time, discrimination grew against Japanese Americans due to the fear that the Japanese living in the country before the war were capable of committing terrorist attacks. In 1942 President Roosevelt issued an executive order giving the War Department authority to evacuate the Japanese from the West Coast and intern them at relocation camps for the remainder of the war. 120,000 Japanese Americans were held until the war ended in 1945. The unfortunate victims of this act were forced to sell their businesses and homes at greatly reduced prices. The monotony of living in the relocation camps was often broken by playing baseball. Some even had family members serving in the American Armed Forces. In 1988 Congress awarded financial restitution to the survivors.

Racial discrimination was also prevalent In the United States Armed Forces at the outset of WWII, with the military being racially segregated. The Tuskegee Airmen were the first African–American military aviators in the United States Armed Forces. Previously, no African–American had been a U.S. military pilot. At left are eight Tuskegee Airmen in front of a P–40 fighter aircraft in 1942. Source: Wikipedia

The Call of Duty

The war effort took its toll on leisure time activities. Although an influx of war movies featuring movie stars such as John Wayne, Anthony Quinn and Spencer Tracey became very popular, other entertainment venues including baseball suffered. Baseball attendance dropped by 25 percent as did the quality of the game. Over 500 Major League and 3,500 Minor League ballplayers were drafted into or joined the armed forces.

LEFT: Ted Williams is inducted into the U.S. Marine Corp. Source: medlibrary.org RIGHT: Joe DiMaggio gets his sergeant's stripes. Source: baseballinwartime.com.

The talent level dropped considerably as the teams employed players who ordinarily would not have made the major leagues. Future Hall of Famers Ted Williams, Stan Musial of the St. Louis Cardinals, hard-throwing pitcher Bob Feller of the Cleveland Indians and Joe DiMaggio, were four key players out of many to put aside their baseball ambitions in order to serve the country. The national past time showed its value on the battle front by often using baseball questions to verify the identification of a U.S. soldier versus a foreign intruder. In an era in which almost all Americans followed baseball, soldiers standing guard would question a suspicious approaching soldier with a question such who batted .406 in 1941 or who hit safely in 56 games? The wrong reply resulted in the arrest of a foreign spy.

Breaking the Color Barrier

Post-war baseball was haunted by discrimination issues. There was mounting pressure from black activists on the owners to end MLB segregation rules. The death of Commissioner Kennesaw Judge Landis, a devout segregationist, in 1944 opened the door for Brooklyn Dodger President Branch Rickey to sign Jackie Robinson in 1945 to a minor league contract with the Montreal farm club. Robinson had been a young star for the Kansas City Monarchs in the Negro League after having been a standout in four sports at UCLA. More importantly to Rickey was the belief that Jackie had the personality, character and fortitude to become the first African American to play Major League Baseball.

Jackie Robinson, courtesy of Negro League Museum.

Robinson joined the Dodgers in 1947 and went on to win the Rookie of the Year Award despite the never-ending harassment he was confronted with in every city the team visited. Later in the same season outfielder Larry Doby of the Cleveland Indians became the first black player in the American League. Jackie led the National League in batting in 1949 and was named the MVP. The integration of baseball set the stage for the civil rights movement to follow in the next decade.

Baseball's Greatest Showman

The late 1940s also welcomed Bill Veeck, the first great promoter of Major League Baseball. His creative ideas and actions in attracting fans and winning baseball games are legendary. As the owner of numerous teams in the 40s and 50s, Veeck ushered in such innovations as fan appreciation night, names on players' uniforms, firework displays at the ball park and the first electronic scoreboard. He also was instrumental in the integration of Major League Baseball by signing Larry Doby and Satchel Paige to the Cleveland Indians.

His best known antic occurred on August 19, 1951. Veeck, then owner of the lowly St. Louis Browns, arranged the stunt using 3 foot 7 inch tall Eddie Gaedel as a pinch hitter against the Detroit Tigers. Eddie was delivered to home plate in a paper mache cake and when he emerged the crowd greeted the little person and his miniature bat with a standing ovation. The pitcher Bob Cain and catcher stood in amazement as he approached the plate. After a consultation on the mound to give Cain time to gain his composure and stop

Bill Veeck (1944), as a U.S. Marine during WWII. Source: United States Marine Corp.

laughing, he walked Gaedel on four consecutive pitches. Veeck had instructed Eddie that under no circumstances should he swing at a pitch. Gaedel trotted down to first base and in his own words "I felt like Babe Ruth." He was replaced with a pinch runner and retired from his baseball career. He was paid $100 for his one at bat appearance. The commissioner of baseball ruled that Veeck violated baseball ethics and such action would not be permitted in future games.

A popular book, *Veeck as In Wreck,* was published in 2001. Considered by many as the zaniest of promoters Veeck set the stage for adding fan entertainment to the game. He was followed in the 1960s by Charlie Findley of the A's and in the 1970s by Ted Turner of the Atlanta Braves. Going to major and minor league ball parks today is similar to taking the kids to the county fair due to the many entertainment features offered at the stadiums.

Baseball and the rest of the country moved into the golden era of the 1950s. General Dwight D. Eisenhower was being urged to run for president, televisions were becoming household items and the surprising 1950 Whiz Kids of the Philadelphia Phillies, led by pitcher Robin Roberts and outfielder Richie Ashburn, won the National League pennant. In New York an era of three fine centerfielders was about to unfold with Mickey Mantle of the Yanks, Willie Mays of the Giants and Duke Snider of the Dodgers. They were often simply referred in writing and later in song as *Mickey, Willie and the Duke.* (see end of chapter six).

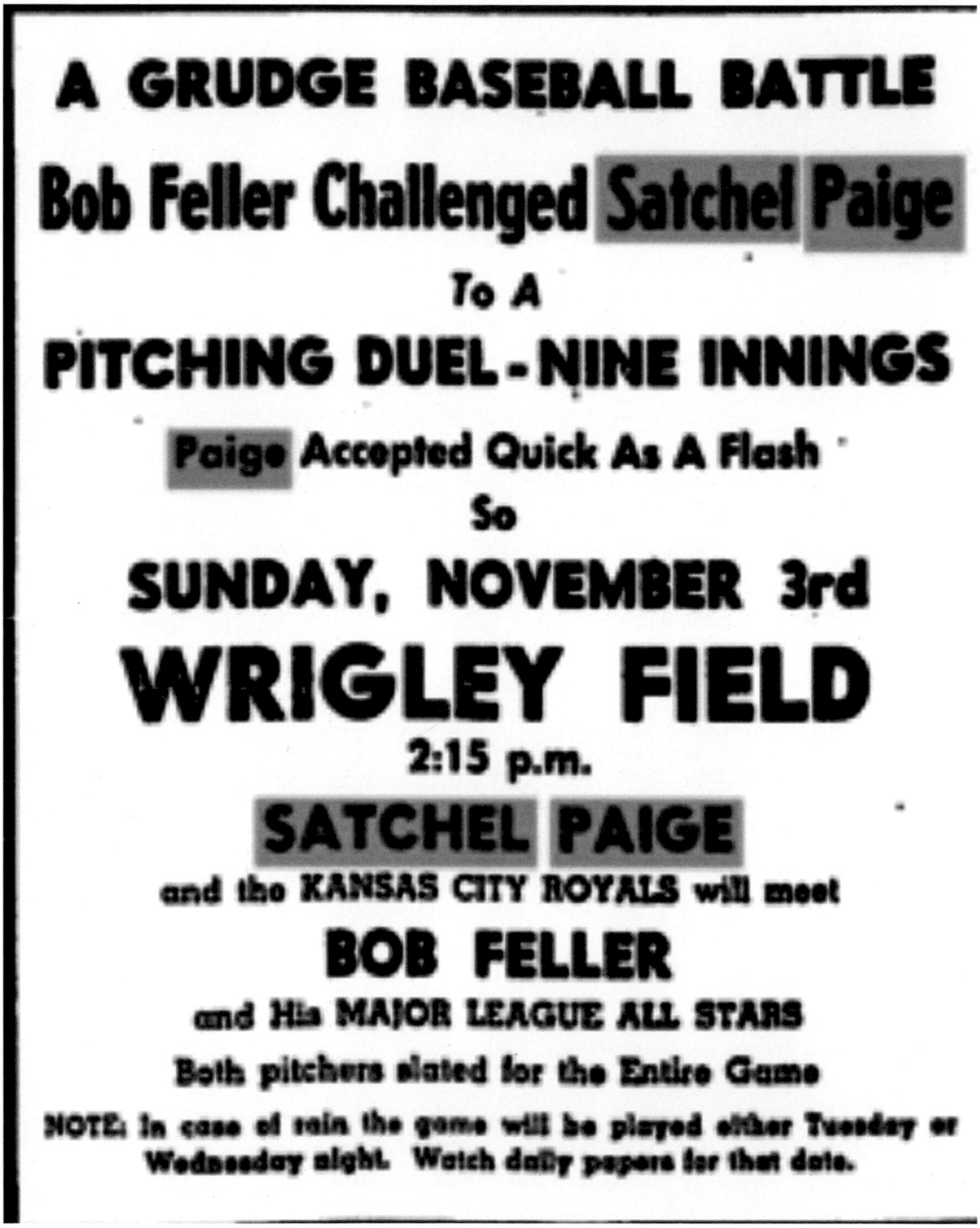

A GRUDGE BASEBALL BATTLE

Bob Feller Challenged Satchel Paige

To A

PITCHING DUEL - NINE INNINGS

Paige Accepted Quick As A Flash

So

SUNDAY, NOVEMBER 3rd

WRIGLEY FIELD

2:15 p.m.

SATCHEL PAIGE

and the KANSAS CITY ROYALS will meet

BOB FELLER

and His MAJOR LEAGUE ALL STARS

Both pitchers slated for the Entire Game

NOTE: In case of rain the game will be played either Tuesday or Wednesday night. Watch daily papers for that date.

Before baseball integrated the All Star exhibition, games were played featuring the Negro League All Stars against the Major League All Stars.

Babe Ruth Dies

Babe Ruth died on August 18, 1948 of cancer. It was a day of sorrow across the United States. Many of the major newspapers devoted their entire front page to stories of his life and career. Grantland Rice, who is widely regarded as the first great sportswriter, took to pen to express the country's sorrow.

"The greatest figure the world of sport has ever known has passed from the field. Game called on account of darkness. Babe Ruth is dead." - Grantland Rice (August 16, 1948)

Game Called by darkness — let the curtain fall.
No more remembered thunder sweeps the field.
No more the ancient echoes hear the call
To one who wore so well both sword and shield:
The Big Guy's left us with the night to face
And there is no one who can take his place.
Game Called — and silence settles on the plain.
Where is the crash of ash against the sphere?
Where is the mighty music, the refrain
That once brought joy to every waiting ear?
The Big Guy's left us lonely in the dark
Forever waiting for the flaming spark.
Game Called — what more is there for us to say?
How dull and drab the field looks to the eye
For one who ruled it in a golden day
Has waved his cap to bid us all good-bye.
The Big Guy's gone — by land or sea or foam
May the Great Umpire call him "safe at home."

Notable Dates and Achievements of the Era

1939 Germany attacks Poland

1941 Japanese attack Pearl Harbor

1944 Normandy invasion

1945 Germany surrenders, United States drops atomic bombs on Hiroshima and Nagasaki, Japan surrenders. President Roosevelt dies.

1947 Taft Hartley Act prohibiting monopolies enacted

1949 NATO formed.

1950 Korean War begins

Literature and Entertainment

1939 Margaret Mitchell's Gone with the Wind sells a million copies in first six months

1936 The movie Mr Deeds Goes to Washington with Jimmy Stewart hits the theatres

Cole Porter and Irving Berlin music are radio highlights

1943 The movie Casablanca wins Academy Award

Benjamin Spock publishes Common Sense of Baby and Child Care (1946)

Beginning of Network television (1948)

Fashions of the Era

Men wore zoot suits, broad brimmed felt hats, pegged trousers and chunky shoes. Hair was long and slicked down. Women wore long coats and haarrache sandals. Pompadour hairdos were the rage.

Baseball Milestones

1941 Dimaggio hits safely in 56 consecutive games, Ted Williams end season with a .407 batting average

1943 The American Girls Professional League founded.

1947 Jackie Robinson and Larry Doby break through Major LEague color line.

1950 The Philadelphia Phillies "Whiz Kids" win the World Series.

FROM TOP: Honolulu Star–Bulletin front page following the Pearl Harbor attack, Nagasaki bombing, author Margaret Mitchell, composer Irving Berlin, and AAGPL ballplayer Gertrude "Tiby" Eisen. MIDDLE OF PAGE: Zoot suits and long coats are the fashions for men and women.

As They Played The Game

Shot heard 'round the world

In 1951 the New York Giants trailed the Dodgers by 13 games on August 11. The Giants proceeded to win 16 games in a row and with one game left in the season they were tied for the pennant. On the last day of the season the Giants handily beat the Braves; but, the Dodgers had to go fourteen innings before Jackie Robinson hit a game winning home run to force a three-game playoff against the Giants for the National League pennant. The Giants won the first game when the Giants outfielder Bobby Thomson, hit a 2-run homer off Dodger starter Ralph Branca.

In Game two the Dodgers evened the playoffs with a 10 to 0 drubbing of the Giants,

(continued to page 58)

1950s: An Age of Affluence?

America was the world leader. The war was behind us; the economy was booming; and jobs were plentiful. There was a tremendous migration to the suburbs and ranch style homes. The G.I. Bill of Rights was passed to assist Armed Forces veterans in purchasing homes and going to college. Televisions were becoming a fixture in most houses and every family seemed to own a car. Women returned to their homes following their war time employment to tend to their familes, although some were finding the return less than fulfilling. Faith in God, country and science was the symbol of the generation. Oh, and there was a young singer named Elvis. Baseball welcomed Mickey, Willie and the Duke.

LEFT: Mickey Mantle and Willie Mays (1968). Source: Desert Sun. RIGHT: Duke Snider (1954). Source: Baseball Digest, September issue.

As They Played The Game (continued from page 57)

setting up a deciding game 3.

The Giants came to bat in the bottom of the ninth inning, trailing 4 to 1. The outlook was dismal but following two singles and a double the score stood at 4 to 2 and the crowd was buzzing. The Brooklyn manager, Chuck Dressen, made a change of pitchers bringing in Ralph Branca, the starting pitcher from game 1, to face Bobby Thomson whose home run had beaten him in game 1. On the second pitch, Thomson hit the ball over the left field fence for a game winning homer.

The fans in the Polo Grounds went crazy as did announcer Russ Hodges with his famous call "the Giants win the pennant, the Giants win the pennant, the Giants win the pennant, the Giants win the pennant." That call is often replayed almost 70 years later. The shared experience given to Thompson and Branca created a friendship between the two and for many years after their retirement the two ball players were hired for speaking events at large conventions.

The decade in baseball started with the "shot heard 'round the world" (see sidebar). The three teams in New York, particularly the Yanks, dominated baseball. Between 1947 through 1960. The Yankees appeared in 11 World Series, The Brooklyn Dodgers seven, and the Giants, two. The three teams were each led by their centerfielders (Mickey Mantle of the Yankees, Willie Mays of the Giants and Duke Snider of the Dodgers) as they challenged each other for New York batting supremacy. All three are in the Hall of Fame. In 1957 Mantle won the Triple Crown by leading the league in batting average, home runs and runs batted in. Although the rivalries created by the three New York teams caused excitement, it was not particularly good for the game as attendance dropped partially due to the lack of competitive balance with other teams. This, plus the growing interest in professional football and basketball and the move to the suburbs away from the cities, caused concern among baseball executives.

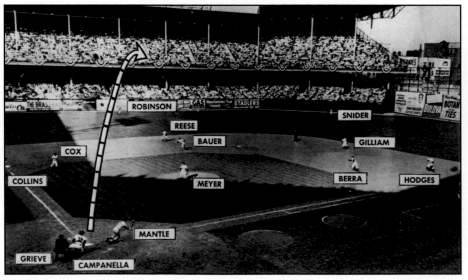

A photograph of Mickey Mantle's grand slam in 1953 off a Russ Meyer pitch in the third inning of the World Series' fifth game at Ebbets Field between the New York Yankees and the Brooklyn Dodgers. Source: The Sporting News Archives.

Westward Bound

In 1953 the dismal attendance at games of the St Louis Browns and the Philadelphia A's forced the teams to relocate to Baltimore and Kansas City respectively. Three years later the Boston Braves moved to Milwaukee. But, the big moves were yet to come. In 1958 Walter O'Malley, owner of the Brooklyn Dodgers, broke the hearts of Brooklynites when he took the team to Los Angeles. Having opened the door for West Coast baseball it was an easy decision for the owner of the New York Giants, Horace Stoneham, to move his team to San Francisco. Baseball had crossed the Mississippi. No longer confined to making long trips by trains, teams could fly easily to any city in the country.

Cold War Era

Outside the ballparks, the perceived Camelot of living in America started to show some cracks. The Cold War between the western allies and the USSR, the Union of Soviet Socialists Republics was a growing concern. By demonstrating that it had created a hydrogen bomb, Russia announced its parity with the United States. The possibility of a nuclear war forced air raid drills in public schools and government facilities. A fear of communism spread across the country like a wild fire. Senator Joseph McCarthy headed up a Senate Committee to investigate communism infiltration in government and society. People lost their jobs if there was any suspicion of communist sympathies. Hollywood was considered a breeding ground for communism which cost many their careers. This went on for three years before exposed as an unfounded intrusion into private lives. McCarthy was censured in 1954 and driven out of office shortly thereafter.

As a result of this fear and the Cold War, the United States went to war in Korea in 1950 when North Korea, supported by Stalin and Russia, invaded South Korea. 33,688 American troops lost their lives in this undeclared war. An armistice was signed that separated Korea into two countries divided by a demilitarized zone in 1952. That separation is still in effect and is a continuing problem almost seventy years later.

Characters of the Game

Not only were the Yankees good they had an array of characters. Two of the most prominent were manager Casey Stengel and catcher Yogi Berra. Both became well known for their imaginative language.

Casey managed the Yanks from 1947 through 1961 after a distinguished playing career with the Brooklyn Dodgers. He was a rather gruff manager often known as "the old professor". When he spoke he had his own special vocabulary which included terms such as:

"Whisky slick" when referring to a baseball player who was a playboy.

"Worm killers" were low-pitched balls.

"Butcher boy" referred to a chopped ground ball.

"Doubleheaded" meant a doubleheader.

"Green pea" was a rookie.

"Hold the gun" was said to the umpire that he intended to change pitchers.

"Plumber" meant the player was a good fielder.

"Road apple" referred to any player he considered a bum.

Stengel's vocabulary and his zany sentences became so well known that a play titled *Stengelese* appeared on Broadway thirty years after his death.

Domestic Dissonance

As The Korean conflict subsided, America turned to a World War II hero to lead the country. "I Like Ike" buttons were being worn by Republicans in 1952 when General Dwight Eisenhower ran for and was elected president. The World War II hero ran as a conservative Republican and handily defeated Democratic Illinois Senator Adlai Stevenson. Richard Nixon was Ike's choice for vice president. His two-term presidency was devoid of military conflicts however the Cold War continued on and the civil rights movement gained momentum. In 1954 the United States Supreme Court ruled against segregation in the Brown versus the Board of Education case. The decision forced an end to laws permitting segregation but the reaction led to massive demonstrations and violence, particularly in the South. In 1955 Rosa Parks refused to give up her bus seat in Montgomery, Alabama, and was forcibly removed by police. This set off a boycott by African Americans of the segregated seating bus system in Montgomery. The effective boycott threatened the city's capacity to continue its transit system. Ultimately the city had to back down and integrate the city buses. This also marked the emergence of the Reverend Martin Luther King, Jr. as a civil rights leader. He was elected as the president of the Southern Christian Leadership Conference and began his crusade for the civil rights of African Americans. His speaking eloquence brought attention to the injustice of segregation and southern Jim Crow laws.

Baseball played an important role in this movement. Black ballplayers stole the spotlight from the whites. Over a 10-year span in the 1950s seven league Most Valuable Player awards went to black ballplayers, including: Willie Mays, Hank Aaron, Larry Doby, Jackie Robinson, Ernie Banks, Roy Campanella and Don Newcombe.

FROM LEFT: Willie Mays and Roy Campanella (1967); World Telegram and Sun photo by William C. Greene, Source: Library of Congress, Prints and Photographs division; Hank Aaron (1960), December issue of Baseball Digest; Ernie Banks (1955), Bowman baseball card; Don Newcombe (1955), September issue of Baseball Digest.

One drawback to the success of baseball's integration was the demise of the Negro League, due to losing its star players. The African American population joined the rest of the nation in following Major League Baseball. Moreover, baseball's popularity continued to grow in Latin America; Cuba was the number one destination for professional baseball players during the winter months.

The civil rights movement was not the only thing that ailed the country. Labor unions were very strong and major strikes threatened the economy. Although President Truman had signed the Taft Hartley Act in 1948 that diluted some of the powers of the unions it had little impact.

Jimmy Hoffa became well known as president of the Teamsters Union which overlooked the working conditions of the trucking industry. The Teamsters along with the AFL-CIO, a conglomeration of many unions, grew to over 20 million members and became a major political force.

The labor problems of the 1950s flowed over into baseball. There was a congressional investigation into Major League Baseball's monopoly status and the legality of its reserve clause. The owners escaped any legal actions but it became apparent that change was coming. The Major League Players Association was formed in 1953 to protect its players and assure its pension plan. It would grow into a powerful union in the next decade. Players were paid on average $10,000- 25,000 with exception of five elite stars. Mickey Mantle, Ted Williams, Stan Musial, Joe Dimaggio and Willie Mays had contracts for $100,000.

Race to the Stars

As the decade was moving to a close the space race began with the Russians launching Sputnik in 1957, the first satellite to orbit the earth. They followed up by sending the first man into space in 1961 when cosmonaut Yuri Gagarin orbited the earth. The United States countered one month later by sending Alan Shepherd into space. President John Kennedy, elected President in 1960, made it an official race by declaring the intention of the USA to land a man on the moon by 1970. In February 1962 astronaut John Glenn orbited the earth in Friendship 7 which sent the message to Russia that we had caught up and would take the lead from thereon.

Baseball Highlights of the Decade

Baseball news stories of the 1950s included the Giants beating the Cleveland Indians in the 1954 World Series, four games to none, despite the fact that the Indians had broken the record for most wins in a 152-game schedule, 111. The record breaking Indians were led by four outstanding pitchers (Bob Feller (HOF), Early Wynn (HOF), Mike Garcia and Bob Lemon) and MVP third baseman Al Rosen. The Giants team featured "Say Hey" Willie Mays, the fleet footed centerfielder who was the most complete player of his era. Willie could run (four times NL stolen base leader), field (12 Gold Glove awards) and hit (.302 lifetime batting average, 660 homeruns). He was selected to 24 All Star Games, won two MVP awards, named Rookie of the Year in 1951 and was inducted into the Hall of Fame in 1979. The "Say Hey" nickname was because of his energetic and gregarious personality. In 1955 the Dodgers finally beat the Yankees in a World Series after having lost to them in 1947, '49, '52 and '53. The dramatic seventh game 2-0 victory by the Dodgers in that series created an hysterical celebration in the borough of Brooklyn.

In 1956 Yankee pitcher Don Larsen did not allow a runner to reach first base and became the only pitcher in baseball history to pitch a

The Cleveland Indians' Four Aces (FROM TOP): Bob Fuller (1953), Mike Garcia (1955), Early Flynn (1933), and Bob Lemon (1955). Source: Bowman Gum.

perfect game in a World Series. The game ended when Larsen struck out pinch hitter Dale Mitchell for the last out in the 2-0 Yankee victory. The 64,519 fans in attendance stood in awe at this historic moment.

A Brush With History

Actually, there were three fewer fans who witnessed this historic strike-out by Don Larsen. Nine-year-old Frank Moye was in the subway with his aunt and 12-year-old brother exiting the ballpark. Frank had been living a child's dream come true. His aunt, a devoted Yankee fan, had promised his 12-year-old brother that if he made his Little League All Star team she would take him and his younger brother to the World Series. They drove straight through from North Carolina in time to see the second game at Ebbets Field and games 3, 4, and 5 at Yankee Stadium.

Adding to the excitement was a photo taken with Mickey Mantle, his aunt's all-time favorite. Having watched all of the first three games the boys were stunned when their Yankee loving aunt suddenly announced in the eighth inning of game 5 that they should leave in order to beat the traffic. Sixty plus years later Frank will tell you he has taken more grief from that story than any other incident in his life.

The 1957 Milwaukee Braves were able to stop the Yankees in a World Series behind the pitching of Warren Spahn and Lew Burdette and young slugger Henry Aaron. Aaron, of course, went on to break Ruth's homerun record when he hit his 715th in Atlanta in 1974. In 1960 Bill Mazeroski, second baseman for the Pittsburgh Pirates, shocked the Yankees with a homerun in the ninth inning of game seven of the World Series to win the championship for the Pirates.

1955 World Series Game One. Source: Sporting News archives. A moment of silence before game one of the 1955 World Series for President Eisenhower, who suffered a heart attack earlier in the day.

The Ghost of Flatbush

LEFT: A postcard of Ebbets Field in Brooklyn, N.Y., depicting the park during its heyday, and right, as the area looked in 2008, after an apartment complex was built on the site.

Imagine living within walking distance of Ebbets Field that night in 1955. Les Shindelman did. His memories of the World Series celebration of 1955 and many other memorable games while growing up as a Dodger fan are seared in his mind like they happened yesterday. Les was a card carrying member of Happy Felton's famous Knothole Gang which allowed him to get into games for seventy-five cents. Happy, a vaudeville player and bandleader, approached Dodger GM Branch Rickey with the idea of a television program that would bring young baseball players together with their idols to learn baseball basics. For seven years (1950-1957, twice each week during the season) Happy would appear at Ebbets Field with Dodger stars such as Jackie Robinson and Peewee Reese playing and practicing baseball with three kids from one of Brooklyn's Little League baseball teams. Knothole Gangs were created to stimulate the interest of youngsters in baseball by offering discounted tickets and became a tradition in many Major League cities. They are still present in a number of Minor League cities.

Les lived in a predominantly Jewish area of Brooklyn where everyone was a Dodger fan. He recalls vividly the celebration that followed the Dodger victory in game 7 of the 1955 World Series against the dreaded Yankees who had beaten them in the 1947, '49, '52 and '53 World Series. Les recalls the excitement of watching Jackie Robinson steal home while unheralded pitcher Johnny Podres pitched a shutout to finally rid the Dodgers of the Yankees hex. Neighborhoods celebrated with gigantic street parties with free food, fireworks and drinks. The Dodgers were a big part of the culture of the town. Many of them lived and worked or operated businesses in Brooklyn during the off season. All Star first baseman Gil Hodges owned a bowling alley.

Ebbets Field was not glamorus like Yankee

Stadium. The contrast of the ballparks illustrated the image of the working class population of Brooklyn versus the wealthier fan base of the the Yankees. There were no fancy electronic scoreboards back then but Les recalls the Schaeffer Beer sign atop the manually operated scoreboard would light up the letter "h" when there was a hit and "e" if there was an error. He recalls fondly his last game at Ebbets with his father in 1957. It was his 11th birthday and his father purchased box seats along the Dodger bullpen. The seats allowed Les to talk Dodger pitcher Roger Craig as he warmed up before the start of the game.

It was heartbreaking to Les and Brooklyn when the Dodgers left town in 1957. Gone were his favorites players – Robinson, the Duke, Don Newcombe, Roy Campanella, and the favorite of the Jewish community, Sandy Koufax. There would be no more sneaking his transistor radio into school to listen to the young announcer Vin Scully call the games. Heartbreak turned to anger as many, including Les, refused to follow or listen to the L.A. Dodgers. The final blow came in 1960 with the demolition of Ebbets Field to make room for an apartment complex.

The baseball world was abuzz, and Brooklyn silent in mourning, when the Dodgers left their home field in 1957 to head out to Los Angeles.

The Brooklyn Dodgers Little League team. Les Shindelman is in the front row, second from left.

The Rise of Little League

The 1950s witnessed the phenomenal growth of Little League baseball throughout America. Little League was founded by Carl Stolz in 1939 in little Williamsport, Pennsylvania, with three teams. Its original growth was limited to Pennsylvania and a few years later moved into New Jersey and New York. By the late 1940s it grew to 92 leagues in the Northeast but when it was featured in an article in the Saturday Post in 1949 the response was overwhelming. Hundreds of cities throughout the country hungered for information on how to join. By 1955 there were leagues in every state in the USA. The Little League World Series was televised and in 1957 a team from Mexico became the first international team to participate in the World Series. The league was an all boys league until 1973.

The growth of Little League baseball has, to a large extent, taken baseball away from kids playing pick-up games in the city streets and school playgrounds. The informal neighborhood teams have been replaced with strict rules, colorful uniforms, professionally designed equipment and adult managers and coaches. It has improved player development with hundreds of graduates playing in the Major League. Many will argue it is better baseball BUT is it more fun?

Trivia Quiz II 1920 – 1960

1. Babe Ruth hit _____ homeruns in his first year as a Yankee?
a. 54
b. 60
c. 27
d. 16

2. Hall of Fame infielder Rogers Hornsby played for _____?
a. White Sox
b. Tigers
c. Pirates
d. Cardinals

3. How old was Satchel Paige the last time he played in the Major Leagues?
a. 42
b. 59
c. 50
d. 63

4. Who threw the pitch that killed Ray Chapman?
a. Christy Mathewson
b. Carl Mays
c. Lefty Grove
d. "Daffy Dean"

5.   Who won the American League MVP award in 1941?
a. Joe Dimaggio
b. Hank Greenberg
c. Eddie Gaedel
d. Ted Williams

6. Who started the All American Girls Professional Baseball League?
a. Bill Veeck
b. Branch Rickey
c. Phillip Wrigley
d. Carolyn Morris

7. Who was the first black ballplayer in the American League ?
a. Satchel Paige
b. Jackie Robinson
c. Larry Doby
d. "Cool Papa" Bell

8. What town was the birthplace for the House of David baseball team?
a. Springfield, Illinois
b. Bar Harbor, Maine
c. Birmingham, Alabama
d. Benton Harbor, Michigan

9. Who gave up Bobby Thomson's "Shot Heard Around the World?"
a. Ronin Roberts
b. Russ Hodges
c. Don Newcombe
d. Ralph Branca

10. Who played centerfield for the 1954 Brooklyn Dodgers?
a. Duke Snider
b. Mickey Mantle
c. Richie Ashburn
d. Willie Mays

11. In 1953 the St Louis Browns moved to what city
a. Milwaukee
b. Baltimore
c. Kansas City
d. Minneapolis

12. Who hit the game winning ninth inning home run in the seventh game of the 1960 World Series?
a. Elston Howard
b. Bill Mazeroski
c. Mickey Mantle
d. Pee Wee Reese

Answers 1. a 2. d 3. b 4. b 5. a 6.c 7. c 8. d 9. d 10. a 11. b 12. b

Talkin' Baseball by Terry Cashman

Songwriter and singer Terry Cashman expressed his nostalgia for the fifties with his record, Talkin Baseball: Willie, Mickey and the Duke.

The Whiz Kids had won it,
Bobby Thomson had done it,

And Yogi read the comics all the while.
Rock 'n roll was being born,
Marijuana, we would scorn,
So down on the corner,
The national past-time went on trial.

We're talkin' baseball!
Kluszewski, Campanella.
Talkin' baseball!
The Man and Bobby Feller.
The Scooter, the Barber, and the Newc,
They knew 'em all from Boston to Dubuque.
Especially Willie, Mickey, and the Duke.

Well, Casey was winning,
Hank Aaron was beginning,
One Robbie going out, one coming in.
Kiner and Midget Gaedel,
The Thumper and Mel Parnell,
And Ike was the only one winning down in Washington.

We're talkin' baseball!
Kluszewski, Campanella.
Talkin' baseball!
The Man and Bobby Feller.
The Scooter, the Barber, and the Newc,
They knew 'em all from Boston to Dubuque.
Especially Willie, Mickey, and the Duke.
Now my old friend, The Bachelor,
Well, he swore he was the Oklahoma Kid.
And Cookie played hooky,
To go and see the Duke.

Well, now it's the 80's,
And Brett is the greatest,
And Bobby Bonds can play for everyone.
Rose is at the Vet,
And Rusty again is a Met,
And the great Alexander is pitchin' again in Washington.

Talkin' baseball!
Carew and Gaylord Perry,
Seaver, Garvey, Schmidt and Vida Blue,
If Cooperstown is calling, it's no fluke.
They'll be with Willie, Mickey, and the Duke.
Willie, Mickey, and the Duke. (Say hey, say hey, say hey)
It was Willie, Mickey and the Duke (Say hey, say hey, say hey)
I'm talkin' Willie, Mickey and the Duke (Say hey, say hey, say hey)
Willie, Mickey, and the Duke. (Say hey, say hey, say hey)
Say Willie, Mickey, and the Duke. (Say hey, say hey, say hey)

Notable Events and Achievements of the Era

!951 Remington Rand Corporation debuts the first commercial digital computer, The UNIVAC (Universal Automatic Computer). CBS introduces the first color television in five USA cities.

1952 Jonas Salk develops the polio vaccine

1953 Korea War ends – 33,329 American lives are lost

1954 Supreme Court rules in Brown versus Board of Education Case that all forms of segregation are unconstitutional.

1955 Ray Kroc opens first MacDonald's

1958 USA launches first satellite, Explorer 1 one year after Russia launched its Sputnik satellite.

1958 Alaska and Hawaii are admitted into the United States. One year later 50 Star flag is dedicated.

1960 President Eisenhower signs the Civil Rights Act of 1960.

Entertainment Headlines

1954 Joe Dimaggio marries actress Marilyn Monroe

1955 Actor James Dean dies in an automobile crash. Disneyland opens in California

1956 Elvis Presley releases his first one million copies solid gold record, Heartbreak Hotel. Actress Grace Kelly marries Prince Ranier III of Monaco.

1959 Rock and Roll stars Buddy Holly, The Big Bopper and Richie Valens die in a plane crash in Clear Lake, Iowa.

Baseball Milestones

1950 Jackie Robinson signs a $35,000 contract, the highest of any Brooklyn Dodger.

1952 Boston Braves pitcher Warren Spahn posts 18 strikeouts in 15-inning game.

1953 Mickey Mantle hits a 564-foot homerun off of Chuck Stobbs of the Washington Senators. Boston Braves move to Milwaukee

1956 Don Larsen pitches only perfect game in a World Series. Don Newcombe becomes the first recipient of the annual CY Young Award.

1958 Dodger Catcher Roy Campanella is paralyzed from the waist down in a car crash.

1959 The Pirates' Harvey Haddix pitches perfect game for 12 innings before losing 1-0 in the 13th inning to the Milwaukee Braves.

1950 Last remaining teams in the Negro Baseball League are disbanded.

From top: Remington Rand computer, McDonald's, Marilyn Monroe and Joe DiMaggio, Elvis Presley.

Baseball and the Arts

Baseball has long been a favorite of the arts and of artists. They are able to capture the spirit and see the value of the sport to America. Pictured here is the artwork of the late Mike Schacht. Mike's favorite subject matter were the old time baseball legends with whom he grew up. His work portrays them in their youth and their heyday. You can see in the eyes of the players and the actions on the field, the intensity and the passion of the athlete.

Mike's work has been featured in Sports Illustrated, ESPN, New York Magazine, and Newsday to name a few. They are also part of the permanent collection in the Baseball Hall of Fame. See more on Mike at www.MikeSchacht.com.

TOP: Ty (the Georgia Peach) Cobb

BELOW: CY Young

SHOELESS JOE JACKSON

ABOVE: Joseph Jefferson "Shoeless Joe" Jackson

LEFT: Satchel Page

ABOVE: Babe Ruth

BELOW: Dizzy Dean

CLOCKWISE FROM TOP: Ted Williams crosses home base;
Willie ("Say Hey") Mays catches up to a long fly ball (1951 World
Series); Mickey Mantle ("the Mick") at Bat;
"Joltin" Joe Dimaggio

CLOCKWISE FROM TOP: Jackie Robinson watches Bobby Thomson score (1951); Duke Snider "The Duke of Flatbush"; Stan "The Man" Musial

"Hammerin" Hank Aaron, after his 751st home run.

Pete Rose, the all-time hits leader

7

Changing Times

(Courtesy of Baseball Almanac)

Yogi Berra became one of the most lovable players in baseball. His squatty appearance was not athletic looking but he looked like a catcher and was a great one. He played in 15 all-star games, won three MVPs, had a lifetime batting average of .285 with 385 home runs. His keen baseball mind made him a very good defensive catcher. The Yankees won pennants 14 of the 17 years that Berra played for them. Following his baseball career, he became a successful manager. He was elected into the Hall of Fame in 1972. But for all of his notable baseball

(Continued to page 80)

The release of Bob Dylan's recording, "The Times They Are a Changin'" in 1964, best illustrates the decade of the sixties. Change was everywhere. Political change happened with the election and assassination of President John F. Kennedy. Societal changes occurred with the civil rights and feminist movements and the Vietnam War. Technological advancements introduced the computer. Music brought in the Beatles and the British invasion. Culturally there was increase in drug use and a more liberal attitude towards sexual behavior. Baseball was not immune from change. It witnessed expansion and reorganization. Although the game remained constant, Major League Baseball's structure went through changes starting in 1961 when it expanded to 10 teams in each league. The American League placed franchises in Minneapolis (Twins) and Los Angeles (Angels). The National League followed suit in 1962 with the addition of the Houston Colt 45s (later to be renamed the Astros) and the New York Mets. The expansion was not an overnight success, as the poor play of the new teams added more imbalance, which hurt attendance. However the new stadiums proved to be an enhancement. The Houston Astrodome became the first air-conditioned domed stadium and was often cited as the eighth wonder of the world. Later in the decade four more teams were added: Kansas City Royals and the Seattle Pilots in the American League, The San Diego Padres and the Montreal Expos in the National League. This allowed each league to create two divisions and hold five game playoffs between the division champs at the end of the season to determine who played in the World Series. This action immediately provided better balance in the competition, increasing attendance and interest.

Wordsmith of the Game (continued from page 79)

skills he is probably best remembered for "Yogi-isms." A few of his famous statements are:

"It ain't over, 'til it's over."

"When you come to a fork in the road, take it."

"Nobody goes there anymore – it's too crowded."

"It's like deja vu all over again."

"Baseball is ninety percent mental and the other half physical."

"A nickel ain't worth a dime anymore."

"Always go to other peoples' funerals, otherwise they won't come to yours."

There is a best-selling book titled *Yogisms* that includes nothing but famous quotes of Yogi Berra. He was not only a great baseball player and noted wordsmith, he participated in the D-Day invasion of Normandy on June 6, 1944. He was the recipient of a medal for bravery from the French government.

The Houston Astrodome, "Eighth Wonder of the World." (1965) Author: Ted Rozumalski. Source: The Sporting News Archives.

Maris' #61*

In 1961, a new Major League record for total number of home runs in a season was set. That year the nation became entranced with a home run battle between two Yankee outfielders, Mickey Mantle and Roger Maris, as they challenged Babe Ruth's 1923 single season record of 60 homeruns. In mid-August, in game number 134, both players were on a path to break Ruth's record. Maris had 53 homers to Mantle's 48; this compared to Ruth's 49 at the same mark in 1923. On September 14, Mantle, with 53 homeruns, conceded the battle because of lingering injuries. Maris charged on. In game 150 he hit number 57 and number 59 on the 154th game. Four games later he hit number 60 and on the last game of the season at Yankee Stadium he broke the single season record by hitting his 61st. BUT ... there was controversy. Did he really break the Babe's record? 1961 also marked the first year of baseball expansion. The American League added two teams in Washington and Los Angeles and increased its schedule to 162 games as opposed to the 154 game limit set in 1901. Since Ruth had hit his 60 homeruns over a 154-game schedule, did Maris really break his record? The Commissioner of Major League, Ford Frick, said "No" and insisted that the record 61st home run have an asterisk beside it to show the number of game discrepancy. That asterisk has since been removed from the record book.

Roger Maris and Mickey Mantle, the "M&M Boys" (1961). Author unknown. Front cover of Baseball Digest, October issue

Cuban Missile Crisis and Dallas

A dark cloud hovered over America in 1962. Newly elected President John F. Kennedy faced a critical situation that Fall when it became clear that Russia was planning to set up missile sites in Cuba. In 1959 Cuba had fallen under the rule of communist dictator Fidel Castro and had become an ally of Russia. The United States would not stand for Russian missile and arms shipments to a foreign enemy only 90 miles from the Florida coast. On October 22, 1962, Kennedy declared that the United States would move forward with a full retaliatory military response against Russia if they proceeded with planned shipments to Cuba. There was at that time an armada of Russian ships headed for Cuba. After calling for military preparedness, Kennedy did not blink an eye as the ships approached the coast of Cuba. In the final moment, Russia Premier Nikita Khrushchev commanded his ships to turn around thus preventing a possible nuclear war. Americans, who were glued to their TVs as the drama unfolded, let out a sigh of relief.

On November 22, 1963, President Kennedy was assassinated by a lone gunman, Lee Harvey Oswald, as his motorcade went through the city of Dallas, Texas. The country went into absolute mourning as they watched continuously the tragedy and funeral unfold on their television sets over the next five days. Vice President Lyndon B. Johnson assumed the presidency. Kennedy's assassination marked the beginning of a dark era in American history.

Cuban Baseball

Professional baseball in Cuba began in 1878. Its popularity spread quickly throughout the country and became the winter home to many major league players in the twentieth century. Growing up in Havana, Pedro Martinez Fonts, whose family ancestors had strong ties to baseball, witnessed the excitement that baseball generated for the Cuban population.

"I left Cuba when I was 12 years old in 1958 dreaming that one day I would be playing shortstop for the NY Yankees. Well, we all know that this dream did not come true, but baseball did provide me with many wonderful memories of my early years in a Cuba that no longer exist.

My grandfather painted a square on a concrete wall and I am told I used to spend hours throwing a rubber or tennis ball against that wall and catching the return. This is when I was 4 or 5 years old.

My father played softball at the Havana Yacht Club and my brother and I would go see him play. When I was 6, they would let me shag balls while they were taking batting practice. At this age I also started to play "organized" ball with the 13-year and under baseball team of the HYC. This was during the summers, during the school year I was bat boy for the 15 and 18 years old team.

Winter baseball was very popular with many American players filling the rosters of the four teams: Almendares, La Habana, Cienfuego and Marianao. We were fans of Almendares and I used to watch and copy a slick fielding shortstop, Willie Miranda, who later played for the Yankees. Other notable

Pedro Martinez Fonts at bat for the Havana Yacht Club

Cuban players were Sandy Amoros who played for La Habana before being traded to Almendares and who made that terrific catch down the left field line in Yankee Stadium to secure the Dodgers World Series win against the Yankees in 1955. All Star outfielder Minnie Minoso of the Chicago White Sox played for Marianao and Camilo Pascual and Pedro Ramos were stellar pitchers for Cienfuegos and Washington Senators.

These games were very lively and I later learned that there was a lot of betting in the stands. I also remember going to see the Cuban Sugar Kings of the International League. This was AAA ball, so it was often we saw players that would later make it in the Major Leagues.

After Castro took over power, the Cuban Sugar Kings were later based out of Miami."

Pedro's family left Cuba in 1958, shortly before the Castro regime took over and banned professional baseball. Amateur baseball is still popular but does not receive the assistance from the government that it provides the national/Olympic sports of boxing and track.

The World Baseball Classic is held every four years and features teams from 16 countries competing for the WBC championship. When the Latin American teams play it offers a glimpse into the excitement of their fan base. The fans wave patriotic flags and banners while loudly singing, chanting and cheering on their teams.

The Vietnam War

President Johnson took a very aggressive stance on the growing communist threat in the country of Vietnam. Both Eisenhower and Kennedy had been keenly aware of the communism threat to the divided countries of North and South Vietnam. American advisers were on the ground aiding the government of South Vietnam as it faced the growing invasion of North Vietnam. President Johnson took a step further. "I am not going to lose Vietnam," he vowed shortly after assuming office. "I am not going to be the President who saw Southeast Asia go the way China went." In August of 1964, Congress approved the Gulf of Tonkin resolution which handed Johnson a mandate to conduct operations in Vietnam as he saw fit. By 1966 there were 380,000 American soldiers in Vietnam. Thus came a 10-year unwinnable war that saw over 50,000 American troops killed and hundreds of thousands of casualties. A divided America watched in horror as the nightly news broadcasts showed the carnage of war. It was the beginning of societal changes that have dramatically changed our lives today. Anti-war demonstrations began in Washington and spread across the country. College student activist groups marched on campuses, and in October 1967 more than 100,000 students marched into D.C. as part of "Stop the Draft Week." The counterculture climate was emboldened by the anti-war music of folksingers such as Pete Seeger's "Where Have All the Flowers Gone" and Bob Dylan's "Blowing in the Wind." The 1968 Democratic Convention in Chicago turned violent as war protestors confronted police using tear gas and clubs. The intensity and number of the demonstrations was undoubtedly a major factor in President Johnson's decision not to run for re-election in 1968. The war did not conclude until 1973 with the capitulation of the South Vietnam Capital City of Saigon to North Vietnam. American troops returned to a seemingly ungrateful nation.

The Civil Rights Movement

Big changes in how society viewed the civil rights of blacks, gays and women was erupting, causing confusion and concern among older Americans. In 1963, the civil rights march brought over 100,000 demonstrators to the Capitol. Martin Luther King, Jr. addressed the crowd with his famous "I Have a Dream" speech. The nation and the politicians started paying serious attention to the plight

As They Played the Game

NY Mets coaches Joe Pignatano, Eddie Yost, and Yogi Berra (1969)

The Amazin' Mets

In 1962 expansion brought baseball back to New York in the name of the New York Mets to replace the Dodgers and the Giants. In the words of Bill Veeck, the previous owner of the lowly St. Louis Browns, upon witnessing the Mets lose game after game, "They are without a doubt the worst baseball team in the history of baseball." Veeck proved to be right. The Mets lost 120 games while winning only 40 but New Yorkers fell in love with the "lovable losers." They were led by the Ole Professor, 71-year-old manager Casey Stengel, the former manager of the champion NY Yankees, who was well known for his zany quotes. It was a team comprised of old ballplayers, well past their prime, and young ball players not ready for the major leagues.

(Continued to page 84)

As They Played the Game (continued from page 83)

New York fans, who were starved for baseball since the departure of their two National League teams to the west coast did not seem to care if they won or not. The cast of characters made it fun. During one of the team's many losing streaks, Casey asked, "Can't anybody play this game?" Another time he asked a battered pitcher if he was tired and after the pitcher said no. Casey replied, "You might not be, but your outfielders are." Outfielder "Marvelous Marv" Thronberry earned his nickname by such plays as getting called out after hitting a triple because he failed to touch neither first or second base on his way to third. The pitching staff had two 20-game losers and a 19-game loser and the league's worse earned run average. They also had the worse team batting average. For the next seven years, the Mets finished either last or next to last until 1969 when they became the "Miracle Mets" by winning the pennant. They proceeded to win the World Series by beating the heavily favored Baltimore Orioles. The song "Meet the Mets" was on the lips of many New Yorkers in the sixties.

of the African Americans. Thanks to MLK, Jr. and his courageous followers, the lives of blacks started to improve. One of his ardent supporters was Jackie Robinson. King recognized Jackie's contribution:

> "Jackie Robinson made it possible for me in the
> first place. Without him, I would never have been
> able to do what I did."
> - Martin Luther King, Jr.

In addition to the civil rights turmoil, the younger generation was opening the door to the drug culture and a more liberal view of sex. Marijuana became the casual drug of choice while drug experimentation with LSD, heroin and cocaine was causing serious concerns and dangers.

(Courtesy of Baseball Almanac)

Players Take a Stand

A notable change in baseball labor relations came in 1966 when labor lawyer Marvin Miller took command of the Major League Players Association. His leadership was dramatic as he forced team owners to negotiate with the union and gained the rights for players to hire agents. These were the beginning steps of the momentum that would grant the players the high salaries they earn today. A key development in the labor war was on October 7, 1969, when Cardinal outfielder Curt Flood refused a trade to the Philadelphia Phillies claiming, "I do not feel I am a piece of property to be bought and sold irrespective of my wishes." Miller agreed to have the union fund a lawsuit against Major League Baseball. Although the lawsuit was dismissed it was to lead to dramatic changes to the rights of baseball players later in the century.

From Hitter's Game to Pitcher's Game

On the field the Yankees, with Mantle, Maris, Yogi Berra and Whitey Ford, continued their dominance in the American League for the first half of the decade. In the National League, the Dodgers, Cardinals and Giants were battling each other for the pennant. Pitching dominated the second half of the decade. Hall of Famers Sandy Koufax and Don Drysdale of the Dodgers, Bob Gibson of the Cardinals and 30-game-winner Denny McClain of the Tigers took center stage.

The Impossible Dream Team

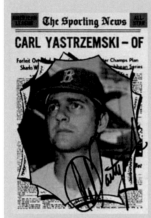

CARL YASTRZEMSKI – OF

(Courtesy of Baseball Almanac)

The final month of the 1967 American League pennant race was arguably the most exciting finish in the history of baseball. As of September 15, three teams, the Red Sox (who had finished in last place in 1966), Twins and Tigers were tied for the American League pennant with identical records of 84 wins and 64 looses. A fourth team, the White Sox, was only 1 ½ games behind the leaders. On Saturday, September 30th, the last weekend of the season, the Twins had moved one game ahead of the Red Sox and Tigers. The White Sox had fallen two games back and needed a miracle to survive. The Tigers were at a disadvantage as they were ending the season with back to back doubleheaders against the Los Angeles Angels while the Red Sox hosted the Twins for two single games. With key homeruns by Carl Yastrzemski and George Scott, the Sox won game one against the Twin 6-4 while the Tigers split their doubleheader against the Angels. This left the Sox and Twins tied for first place with the Tigers a half game back. The White Sox were eliminated and the Tigers would have to sweep their final twin bill to force a playoff with either the Twins or Red Sox.

In Boston, both teams pitched their best for the final game. The eventual Cy Young award winner Jim Lonborg (21-9) for the Red Sox was pitted against 20 game winner Dean Chance of the Twins. Errors bit the Sox as the Twins scored two early runs and were feeling confident as Chance mowed down the Sox allowing just four hits over the first five innings. But in the sixth, pitcher Lonborg laid down a bunt single to start the inning and Chance fell apart. Three singles, two wild pitches and an error allowed the Red Sox to score five runs They went on to win 5-3. However, the suspense was not over. The Tigers won their first game and would tie for the pennant if they completed the doubleheader sweep. The entire Red Sox nation crowded around their televisions to watch the second and final game of the season. On the mound for the Tigers was the young, hard throwing Denny McLain (20-14). However, Denny did not have it that day and the Angels blasted out an 8-5 win allowing the Red Sox to complete their "Impossible Dream season."

A side note to this story is how Triple Crown winner outfielder Carl Yastrzemski led the Red Sox to their improbable last to first place finish. For the season he batted .326 with 44 home runs and 126 runs batted in and won the Gold Glove for fielding excellence. In that final month of the season Yaz batted .417 with nine homeruns and 26 runs in the final 27 games. He went 7 for 8 in those pressured filled final two games.

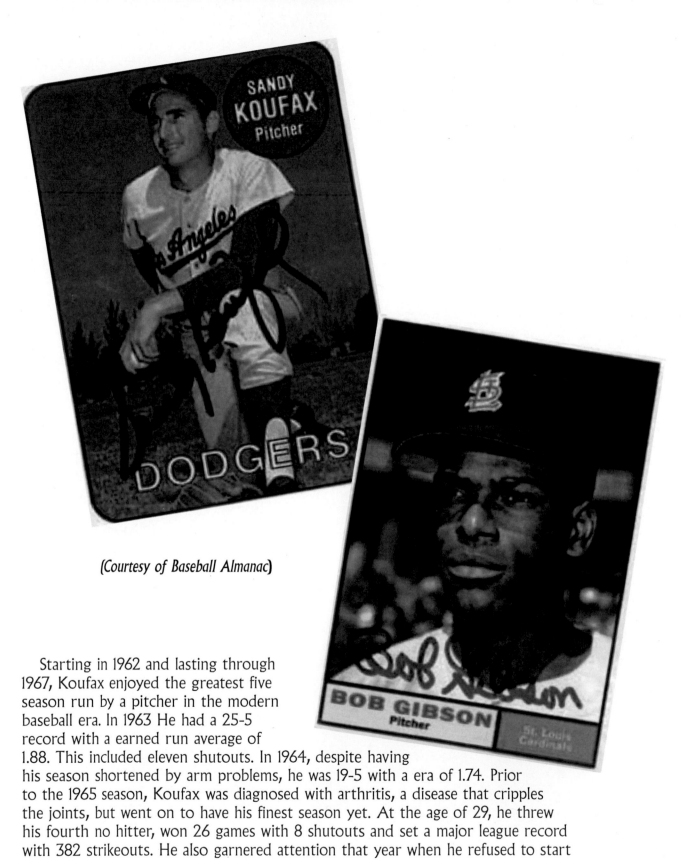

(Courtesy of Baseball Almanac)

Starting in 1962 and lasting through 1967, Koufax enjoyed the greatest five season run by a pitcher in the modern baseball era. In 1963 He had a 25-5 record with a earned run average of 1.88. This included eleven shutouts. In 1964, despite having his season shortened by arm problems, he was 19-5 with a era of 1.74. Prior to the 1965 season, Koufax was diagnosed with arthritis, a disease that cripples the joints, but went on to have his finest season yet. At the age of 29, he threw his fourth no hitter, won 26 games with 8 shutouts and set a major league record with 382 strikeouts. He also garnered attention that year when he refused to start game 1 of the World Series, citing the conflict with the Jewish holiday of Yon Kippur. In his final season, 1967, Sandy won 27 games, with an era of 1.73, 313 strikeouts and along with teammate Don Drysdale led the Dodgers to their third World Series in five years. On November 18th 1966, the 30-year-old southpaw announced his early retirement due to concerns that the ever present arthritis in his arm would lead to permanent injury. In 1972, he became the youngest player ever to be elected into the Hall of Fame.

Koufax's greatest competitor was Bob Gibson of the St. Louis Cardinals. In 1968, the fire balling Gibson won 22 games with 13 shutouts while striking out 218 batters and recording a 1.12 ERA (the lowest ever posted). In 1968, due to the dominance of pitchers like Koufax, Drysdale, Gibson and McClain, batting averages had fallen to an all-time low of .237. Commissioner Bowie Kuhn was forced to shorten the strike zone and lower the height of the pitching mound to satisfy the fans desire for more offense. The move also pleased sluggers like Hank Aaron, Willie Mays, Frank Robinson, Reggie Jackson and Carl Yastrzemski.

The Old Guard was Fading...

The mid-sixties saw the fall of the Yankees. Having dominated baseball for the better part of forty years the Yankees fell from first place in the American League in 1964 to dead last in 1965 26 ½ games behind the Baltimore Orioles followed by a ninth place finish in 1966. Mantle could hardly run on his chronic bad knees and retired along with pitcher Whitey Ford and catcher Yogi Berra. Other notable retirees of the era included Ted Williams, Stan Musial, Warren Spahn and Sandy Koufax. They were replaced by such stars as outfielder Frank Robinson, catcher Johnny Bench and Pete Rose of the Cincinnati Reds, Reggie Jackson and pitcher Catfish Hunter of the Oakland A's, outfielder Carl Yastrzemski of the Red Sox and outfielder Roberto Clemente.

"I can't play anymore (retirement press conference on
March 1, 1969). I can't hit the ball when I need to. I can't
steal second when I need to. I can't go from first to third
when I need to. I can't score from second when I need to.
I have to quit."

-Mickey Mantle

...and the Beat Goes On

The country's problems of the sixties were never ending. On April 4, 1968, civil rights leader the Reverend Martin Luther King, Jr. was assassinated in Memphis, Tennessee. Adding to the grief of the nation, two months later presidential candidate Robert Kennedy, brother of John, was assassinated in Los Angeles. This was followed by the fatal shooting on May 4, 1970 of four student protestors on the campus of Kent State University by National Guardsmen who were called in to quell an anti-war rally.

About the only uplifting event of the era was the fulfillment of President Kennedy's vow to put a man on the moon when, on July 20, 1969, Neil Armstrong took "one giant leap for mankind" as he set foot onto the moon. The nation looked forward to better times in the seventies, unaware of the continuation of the war and the coming Watergate scandal in the White House.

Great Americans and News of the Era

1960 John F. Kennedy elected as President

1962 Cuban Missile Crisis

1963 President Kennedy assassinated, Lyndon B. Jonson assumes the presidency, civil rights march on Wasington, D.C. (Martin Luther King delivers his "I Have a Dream" speech.)

1964 President Johnson signs the Civil Rights Act. Gulf of Tonkin Resolution authorizes use of military action in Vietnam. Beatles arrive for first tour of America.

1965 Race riot on Watts District of Los Angeles

1967 100,000 Vietnam protesters march into Washington, D.C.

1968 Martin Luther King and Robert Kennedy are assassinated, riots at Democratic National Convention in Chicago, Richard Nixon elected President

1969 Apollo 11 lands on the moon, Neil Armstrong declares, "One step for man, one giant step for mankind."

Popular movies, music and fashions

Movies - *2001 Space Odyssey, Sound of Music, Psycho, The Graduate, and To Kill A Mockingbird*

Music - The Beatles, Rolling Stones, Diana Ross and the Supremes, the Temptations, Roy Orbison, Sonny and Cher

Fashions - Hippie look, Flower Child and love beads, the Jackie Kennedy look, bell bottom jeans

Baseball Milestones

1961 Roger Maris breaks Babe Ruth homerun record

1962 Buck O'Neil becomes first African American major league coach

1965 First free agent draft, Warren Spahn retires with 363 wins — record for a left-handed pitcher

1966 Pitcher Tony Cloninger hits two grand slam homeruns in one game

1967 Carl Yastrzemski named American League MVP and wins Triple Crown

1968 Tigers pitcher Denny McLain wins 31 games

1969 Mickey Mantle retires

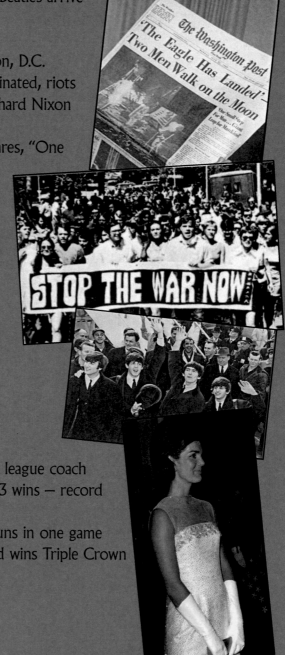

FROM TOP: Washington Post front page story on the Apollo 11 landing, FAU students at an anti-war demonstration, the Beatles, Jacqueline (Jackie) Kennedy.

8

Civil Rights for Ballplayers

Roberto Clemente, left, and Thurman Munson (Courtesy of Baseball Almanac)

Adding to the pain of the Vietnam War was the political scandal of the century. On June 17, 1972, five burglars broke into the Democratic National Committee headquarters located in the Watergate Hotel in Washington D.C. Their objective was to steal information regarding the political plans of the Democrats for the upcoming presidential campaign. The group was directed by former CIA agent Gordon Liddy. He was hired by the power brokers of the Republican Party. The two-year investigation into who authorized the burglary eventually led to the top officials of the White House, including President Nixon. Rather than go through an impeachment trial, Nixon submitted his letter of resignation on August 8, 1974, and turned the presidency over to Vice President Gerald Ford.

Tensions Between Owners and Players

(Courtesy of Baseball Almanac)

Baseball was having its own problems throughout the seventies. The Major League Players Association (MLPA), continued to grow in strength under the leadership of Marvin Miller. The 1969 law suit of outfielder Curt Flood of the St. Louis Cardinals and its outcome plagued baseball for the remainder of the century. His refusal to accept a trade to the Philadelphia Phillies went to the Federal District Court in New York. Although denied, the publicity that was attracted opened the door for a fight to end the reserve clause. In 1972, players held a 13-day strike in

On December 23, 1972, a 6.3 earthquake hit the center of the capital city of Nicaragua, Managua. More than 5,000 people were killed and over 300,000 were left homeless. Assistance was slow in coming, and in many cases supplies were pirated and never reached their intended destination. In Puerto Rico, 38-year-old Roberto Clemente, Pittsburgh Pirate All Star outfielder and future Hall of Fame member, took it upon himself to organize a relief effort. He and a small group of friends loaded a private plane with supplies and took off on December 31 to Managua. The plane never arrived. Due to the plane being over loaded,

(Continued to page 90)

Baseball Tragedies (continued from page 89)

Clemente and his crew crashed almost on takeoff. There were no survivors.

To recognize Clemente's bravery he was elected into the Hall of Fame the following year having been excused from the five-year mandatory waiting period. He was the first Latin American baseball player to be enshrined into the Hall. Roberto was a 15-time All Star, a MVP, a four-time National League batting champion, and a twelve-time winner of the Gold Glove award for his fine fielding. He had a lifetime batting average of .317 and accumulated 3,000 base hits. Each year Major League baseball honors the National League player who makes the greatest charitable contributions to their community with the Roberto Clemente Award. A statue of Roberto Clemente greets fans as they enter PNC Park, the home of the Pittsburgh Pirates.

Seven years later, a private plane crash took the life of Thurman Munson. Munson, a 32-year-old, was the captain and catcher for the New York Yankees. In his shortened Major League Baseball career, he was named Rookie of the Year, earned an MVP award, won three Gold Glove Awards, and was named to seven All Star teams. His locker room locker stands on display in the New York Yankee Museum.

protest of the clause. In 1973, two players, Andy Messersmith of the Dodgers and Dave McNally of the Orioles, following the lead of Curt Flood opted to sit out a season. This was the only way at the time to gain free agency and the right to sell their services to the team of their choice. Messersmith was rewarded with a 3-year, million-dollar contract with the Atlanta Braves and its owner Ted Turner. McNally decided to retire. Thus the beginning of the high-salaried baseball player. In 1976, the MLPA negotiated a basic agreement with ownership that granted free agency to any player with six years of major league experience.

The tension did not stop there. In 1981, as a reaction to the owners attempting to place a ceiling on player salaries, the players went on strike again for six weeks and forced cancellation of 713 games. The strike was very costly to players and owners but the outcome produced great gains in future player salaries and benefits. Between 1970 and 1981, player salaries increased from an average salary of $25,000 in 1970 and to $185,000 in 1981. There was no shedding of tears for the owners as their wallets also got fatter thanks to the increasing revenues received from television networks and rising record attendance. Ball players gained the civil rights they fought for since the start of organized baseball in 1876.

Societal Upheavals

Society's civil rights movement of the sixties spread quickly to women and the gay community. Both groups held demonstrations and parades in order to gain recognition of the discrimination against them. In 1973, the Supreme Court ruled in favor of the Roe v. Wade case which granted women the right to choose abortion as an alternative to giving birth.

There was also an active movement by environmentalists to save the planet. The year 1970 marked the first Earth Day celebration. In 1979, the nation shuttered with news of a nuclear reaction meltdown at the Three Mile Island nuclear power plant outside of Harrisburg, Pennsylvania. Many of the environmental destruction fears expressed by Rachel Carson in her bestselling book *Silent Spring* were becoming real.

Jimmy Carter took the presidential reins from Gerald Ford in 1976. He was unable to stop a slumping economy. Inflation was rampant, there were gas shortages and jobs were threatened by deindustrialization due to growing technology. Ironically, as the baseball union grew in strength, the labor unions weakened. Less industrial jobs meant less union members. Carter's greatest moment was the Camp David Accord in which he was able to bring President Anwar Sadat of Egypt together with Prime Minister Menachen Begin of Israel to sign an agreement of peace with the two antagonistic countries. His lowest point was in 1979 when 52 American diplomats and their staffs were taken hostage by Iran and held for 444 days. They were not released until Ronald Reagan took over as President in 1981.

Baseball Divisions and Subdivisions

Baseball continued its upward movement through more relocation and expansion. In 1972, the Seattle Pilots became the Milwaukee Brewers and Washington Senators became the Texas Rangers. In 1977, new teams were granted to Seattle (Mariners) and Toronto (Blue Jays). In 1973, a big change occurred in the American League with the creation of the designated hitter (DH) position. It was designed to boost offense by allowing proven hitters to bat for weak hitting pitchers. The National League refused to go along, believing that the strategies employed by having the pitcher hit for himself made the game more interesting. The stance of each league has not changed and it is a lively discussion today between fans of differing opinions.

On the field, the creation of league subdivisions helped to correct the imbalance of competition. The first half of the seventies was all about the young Oakland A's as they won three consecutive World Series behind the pitching of Catfish Hunter and Vida Blue. A young slugging outfielder named Reggie Jackson led their offense. In the mid-seventies, the Cincinnati Reds became known as the Big Red Machine. Led by the all time hits leader Pete "Charlie Hustle" Rose, future Hall of Famers second baseman Joe Morgan and catcher Johnny Bench they wreaked havoc on opposing pitchers. They won the 1975 World Series by outdueling the Boston Red Sox.

Many declare game six of the '75 series as the most exciting World Series game ever played. In a back-and-forth game with Boston trailing 6-3 in the eighth inning, pinch hitter Bernie

(*Courtesy of Baseball Almanac*)

Carbo hit a 3-run homer to tie the game. Three exciting innings later, after both teams missed numerous opportunities to score, Boston catcher Carlton Fisk hit one out of the park to win the game. The next day the Reds were victorious 4 to 3 to win the championship.

George Steinbrenner

George Steinbrenner (1973)

George Steinbrenner took control of the New York Yankees in 1973 as the majority owner. Steinbrenner brought a new style of management to Major League Baseball. Known as "The Boss," he ushered in an era of free spending and control management that brought the Yankees back to the forefront of baseball. His win-at-any-cost attitude was supported by his lavish spending on free agents.

An unpredictable force, Steinbrenner was not easy to work for. During his first 23 seasons, he employed 20 managers, which included the firing and rehiring of manager Billy Martin five times. He was a tireless worker who expected the same from his employees. The staff grew used to middle-of-the-night phone calls to discuss operations and being constantly threatened to be fired. His management style was not limited to staff as players faced strict discipline for violations of any number of rules that were imposed including strict policies on facial hair and length of hair. He once ordered star first baseman, Don Mattingly, benched for refusing to trim his hair.

No matter how difficult the man could be, it worked on the field. Steinbrenner bought the lowly Yanks for $10 million and immediately started to return them to their legendary status. He spent freely on free agents. Early on he added Hall of Fame players, pitcher Jim "Catfish" Hunter, and outfielders Reggie Jackson and Dave Winfield. Later such stars as pitcher Roger Clemens and Hall of Fame outfielder and speedster Rickey Henderson were picked up to continue building the Yankee dominance. During his tenure, the Yankees won 11 pennants and seven World Series.

There were numerous ego conflicts between Steinbrenner and his star players. Dave Winfield, who had signed a $10-million contract in 1981 (at the time was the largest in baseball), sued the Yankees for failure to follow through on an agreed upon $300,000 contribution that was to be made to his foundation. Steinbrenner took offense and hired a mafia-associated thug to dig up dirt on Winfield. When this association arrangement was uncovered MLB Commissioner Fay Vincent banned Steinbrenner from the daily operations of the team for three years.

That was not the first time Steinbrenner had been banned. In 1974, Commissioner Bowie Kuhn permanently banished Steinbrenner from running the Yankees after he was convicted and fined in court for making illegal campaign contributions to President Richard Nixon. Later, Kuhn commuted the sentence after 15 months.

There was never a dull moment under Steinbrenner's management style. His larger than life character was depicted for many years on the very popular television show *Seinfeld*. George died in 2010. At he time of his death, the Yankee franchise was valued at over one billion dollars. In consideration of the ten-million-dollar original investment, a phenomenal rate of return.

Baseball Milestones of the 1970s

There were many individual achievements. Hall of Famers outfielder Frank Robinson and third baseman Brooks Robinson (not related) led the Orioles to two World Series appearances. Frank Robinson was a two-time MVP and only player to win the award in both leagues. He became the first black manager in Major League history when he became a player manager for the Cleveland Indians in 1975. Willie McCovey, first baseman for the San Francisco Giants, succeeded Willie Mays as the team's slugger. On April 8, 1974, "Hammerin" Hank Aaron hit his 715th home run off of Dodger pitcher Al Downing to break Babe Ruth's all time record for home runs. Pitcher Nolan Ryan of the California Angels won the American League Cy Young award in 1973 by throwing two no-hitters and striking out 383 batters. Just as amazing was the season Steve "Lefty" Carlton had for the last place Phillies in 1972. He won 27 games for a team that only won 59. Tom Seaver displayed his excellent pitching for the Mets and won a Cy Young Award in 1973. Two hitters threatened to break the .400 batting average mark. Outfielder Rod Carew of the Minnesota Twins, who won four consecutive batting titles, hit .388 in 1977. George Brett, third baseman of the Kansas City Royals came even closer by batting .390 in 1980 when he led the team to their first World Series. Unfortunately they lost the series to the Phillies who were led by Hall of Fame third baseman Mike Schmidt.

FRANK ROBINSON

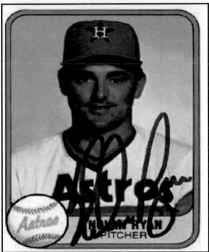

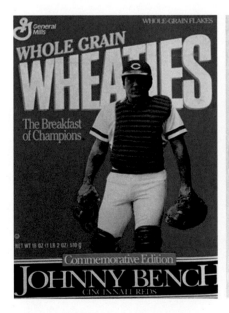

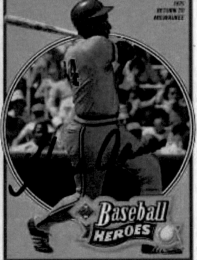

Hank Aaron

All in the Family

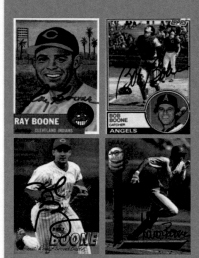

CLOCKWISE FROM TOP: Ray Boone,
Bob Boone, Bret Boone, and Aaron Boone
(Courtesy of Baseball Almanac)

Throughout the history of baseball there have been over 200 second generation family players. Most notably of recent times HOF Ken Griffey Jr. followed his dad, and Barry Bonds followed his dad Bobby. But, there have been only a very few three generation family players.

In 1972 Bob Boone, a highly regarded catcher, followed his dad Ray into the major leagues. Bob who played for the Phillies of the National League and later for the Los Angeles Angels of the American League was a four time All Star. During his 18-year career he was awarded seven gold gloves for his fine defensive skills. He out did his infielder dad who played for six teams from 1948 to 1960 appeared in two All Star games and led the American League in RBIs in 1955. Both were very talented ball players but are better known for what was to follow.

Bob's oldest son Bret played in the major leagues from 1992 to 2005 as an infielder for the Seattle Mariners. In his thirteen-year career Bret appeared on three All Star games, won four gold gloves and two Silver Slugger awards as the best hitting player for his position. In 2001 Bret set a Seattle Mariners record for a second baseman, when he hit 37 homeruns, with 141 RBIs and a .331 batting average.

But the Boone family was not through yet. In 1997 Bob's younger son, Bret's brother, Aaron, joined the family heritage as a Yankee infielder. Although much of his twelve-year career he served as a utility infielder for six different teams, he was selected as an All Star in 2003, making him the fourth Boone to play in an All Star game. In 2018, Aaron was named as manager of the New York Yankees.

Three generations is amazing but hold on, there may be more coming. In 2017, the Washington Nationals selected Bret's oldest son in the baseball draft. If he makes the major leagues the Boone family would become the only four-generation family to play Major League Baseball. Who knows how many siblings and cousins might come along with and after Jake?

It makes you wonder, where did all this athleticism come from? Perhaps it has something to do with the fact that Boone family is in the direct family ancestry of Daniel Boone, the famous Kentucky pioneer.

There have been over 350 siblings in the major leagues playing at the same time. To name a few: the Dimaggio boys, Joe (HOF), Dom and Vince, pitching brothers included Phil (HOF) and Joe Niekro, Jim and Gaylord Perry (HOF) and Dizzy (HOF) and Paul (Daffy) Vance of the Gashouse Gang of the 1930s Cardinals.

There were several brothers who played on the same team. But only one time have three brothers played on the same team at the same time. In 1963 Felipe, Matty and Jesus Alou manned the outfield for the San Francisco Giants versus the New York Mets.

Some things are destined to be.

Rick Monday: An All-American Ballplayer

Rick Monday

read "RICK MONDAY-YOU MADE A GREAT PLAY."

The flag was presented to Rick on May 4, 1976 "Rick Monday Day" at Wrigley Field. He still has the flag despite offers reportedly of a million dollars for it. "If you're going to burn the flag, don't do it around me. I have been to too many veterans hospitals and seen too many broken bodies of guys who tried to protect it," he stated. Monday served with the Marine Corps Reserve.

It was April 25, 1976 and America was celebrating its Bicentennial. The Vietnam War was finally over but the country was still far from tranquil. At the Dodger Stadium, Rick Monday was covering centerfield for the Chicago Cubs in the bottom of the fourth inning when two protestors ran into left center field carrying an American flag along with a can of lighter fluid. Dodger announcer Vin Scully exclaimed, "It looks like he's going to burn the flag." As they spread the flag out on the field and lit a match, Monday dashed over and grabbed the flag from them. Carrying the flag, he ran to the infield as the crowd cheered him on. The two protestors, a father and his eleven-year-old son, were escorted from the field by police. When Monday came up to bat in the top of the fifth, he was greeted with a standing ovation and a flashing sign on the scoreboard that

(Courtesy of Baseball Almanac)

Great Americans and News of the Era

Achievements and Events of the Era

1970 Monday Night Football debuts with Howard Cosell, Don Meredith and Keith Jackson serving as play-by-play commentators and analysts. Kent State tragedy in which four student protestors are fatally shot by National Guardsmen.

1972 Watergate break in results in the apprehension of five burglars attempting to steal information from the National Democratic headquarters. Floppy disks are on the market.

1973 U.S. Supreme Court rules in favor case of Roe v. Wade legalizing abortion. First cell phones are created.

1974 President Richard Nixon resigns as a result of the Watergate investigation. Gerald Ford assumes presidency. Charles Lindbergh dies.

1975 Saigon falls, all US troops return home.

1976 America celebrates its bicentennial.

1979 Accident at Three Mile Island Nuclear Plant causes unrest in regards to danger of radiation spills.

1980 John Lennon is fatally shot.

CLOCKWISE FROM TOP:

The Dyna TAC cellphone, a woman wearing a mini skirt, Star Wars logo, and the Jackson Five

Popular Movies, Music and Fashions

Movies - *Star Wars, One Flew Over the Cuckoo's Nest, The Sting, Jaws, Animal House, All the President's Men*

Music - Country Rock, The Jackson Five, Glen Campbell, Janis Joplin, James Taylor, The Allman Brothers, Punk Rock, John Denver

Fashion - Miniskirts, boots, hot pants, pastel colors, disco fashions, leisure suits for men, Farah Fawcett hairstyle

Baseball Milestones

1971 Pirates play with an all minority lineup; Satchel Paige elected to the Hall of Fame; Roberto Clemente reaches 3,000 hits; Steve Carlton wins 27 games for last place Phillies.

1973 Steinbrenner takes control of the New York Yankees; American League adopts the designated hitter position.

1974 Frank Robinson become first African American manager; Mets / Cards play a 25-inning game lasting 7 hours and 25 minutes.

1977 Reggie Jackson gains nickname as Mister October after hitting three homeruns in a World Series games.

1980 KC Royal third baseman George Brett bats .390; Hank Aaron protests against the treatment of black player retirement pensions.

The Longest Game Ever Played

The 1,740 fans who showed up to see the Pawtucket Red Sox take on the Rochester Red Wings had no idea what they were getting into. On a chilly Easter Eve evening, April 19, 1981, the two AAA minor league teams took the field. After nine innings, the game was tied 1-1 and moved into extra innings. For the next 11 innings, neither team could score a run until the Red Wings scored a run in the top of the 21st inning to make it 2-1. However, in the bottom of the inning, Pawtucket's future Major League Hall of Fame third baseman Wade Boggs lined a hit to the outfield to tie the game. The players groaned. Boggs later commented, "I didn't know if the guys on my team would hug me or slug me." The game went on,

(Continued to page 98)

9

Hollywood and Baseball

In 1981 Governor of California and movie star Ronald Reagan moved into the White House. Candidate Reagan had campaigned on turning around a bad economy. As president, Reagan imposed his trickle-down economics theory which cut taxes in order to increase consumer spending and expand employment opportunities. It did not occur overnight but eventually the economy turned upwards. Reagan gained a reputation as a great communicator and strong leader. He took on the nation's air traffic controllers when 13,000 controllers walked off the job. The walk off was illegal because they were government contract employees who did not have the right to strike. The President went on television and made the announcement that any controllers not reporting to work within 48 hours would be fired. Eleven thousand controllers called the President's bluff and were fired. Three thousand supervisors joined 2,000 non-striking employees and 1,000 military air control tower operators to keep the airlines running. It was hectic and some airlines were forced to cancel approximately 50 percent of their flights, but there were no airplane accidents. Six months later a new cadre of professionally trained civilian air control tower operators had reported to work.

The Great Communicator

President Reagan also gained the respect of baseball fans. One of his first jobs was acting as a sports broadcaster for WHO radio station in Des Moines, Iowa from 1934-1937. In this capacity, he was the local broadcaster for the Chicago Cubs. These were the days before modern communication, so local broadcasters relayed the action by reading play-by-play from a

The Longest Game Ever Played (continued from page 97)

the temperature dropped. Players were setting fire to baseball bats and benches to keep warm. There was no food to be found. They continued to play until the League President called the umpires from his home and demanded the game be paused after 32 innings. It was 4:07 a.m. and 19 fans were still on hand at McCoy Stadium. The game was to resume three days later.

A sellout crowd of 5,746 fans showed up to witness the ending of the longest game in baseball history. It did not last long. In the bottom of the 33rd inning, Pawtucket's Dave Koza drove in the winning run just 18 minutes into the delayed game. Pawtucket won 3-2 in 33 innings in a game that lasted 8 hours and 25 minutes.

There were many game and individual records set. For example, Rochester' Outfielder Dallas Williams went 0 for 13 in 15 at bats; Dave Ruppert caught 31 consecutive innings for the Red Wings; and Pawtucket's Russ Lambee struck out seven times.

There is a ball from the game on display at the Hall of Fame in Cooperstown.

Ronald Reagan as radio announcer.
Courtesy Ronald Reagan Library.

teletype machine. If the relay got interrupted the announcer would often adlib as to what was happening on the field, usually by calling foul ball over and over again until the machine was operating again. Reagan often claimed this was the start of his learning how to act. For baseball fans, it was appropriate to have a Hollywood President — after all baseball and Hollywood were friends for many years. The national pastime has been featured in award winning films since the days of Ruth and Gehrig. The eighties brought a slew of popular baseball films to the theatres. In 1984 Robert Redford starred in *The Natural* as a superman type of slugger. It was followed in the same year by the romantic comedy of life in the minors, *Bull Durham*. Then, in 1989, Kevin Costner starred in the much loved *Field of Dreams*. Also, baseball celebrities appeared often in television programs and of course, often in commercials endorsing products.

A Carousel of Commissioners

Due to baseball's ongoing labor relations problems, the Commissioner of Baseball position went through four leaders during the eighties. Bowie Kuhn held the title from 1969-1984 and was the Commissioner during the Curt Flood proceedings. He had ongoing conflict with Marvin Miller of the Major League Baseball Players Association (MLBPA). His rule was contentious and owners placed much of the union victories at the feet of Kuhn forcing his resignation in 1984.

Peter Ueberroth was elected by the owners to take the reins. Ueberroth was coming off a successful leadership of the 1984 Los Angeles Summer Olympic Games in which he received *Time Magazine's* Man of the Year recognition. But he also was not able to quell the momentum of the union. He had a number of clashes with the MLBPA including a damaging suit brought against the owners, accusing them of collusion in bidding for free agents. That was enough for him to step down at the

FROM TOP LEFT: Baseball Commissioners Bowie Kuhn (1982), Author: MLB; Peter Ueberroth (Date and author unknown); A. Bartlett Giamatti (Date and author unknown); and Fay Vincent, still image taken from a film about the life and times of Yankee owner George Steinbrenner, Author: New York Yankees and MLB

Ozzie Smith, Author: John Mena

end of his 5-year term.

Bart Giamatti, a former President of Yale University, eagerly accepted the position on 1989. Giamatti was a lifelong baseball fan and had served as Commissioner of the National League since 1986. He was also a noted author of baseball books and publications. His most noted action was issuing a lifetime Major League banishment of All Star player and manager Pete Rose for gambling activities. Rose admitted that during his role as manager of the Philadelphia Phillies he bet on games although he claimed that none of the games involved the Phillies. Commissioner Giamatti died of a heart attack in September of 1989 just six months after assuming the office.

The Deputy Commissioner, Faye Vincent, assumed the Commissioner's job upon Giamatti's untimely death.

Extraordinary Players of the Eighties

In the mid-eighties, baseball fans were being entertained by two future Hall of Famers known for their speed and agility. Ozzie Smith (aka The Wizard of Oz) was a shortstop for the St Louis Cardinals. The Wizard played for 18 seasons, made 15 All Star teams, won 13 consecutive gold gloves for fielding excellence, and stole 580 bases. He was a fan favorite not only for his skill on the field but also for his ability to perform a total back flip when he would take the field. Another young player who was drawing attention was speedy Rickey Henderson of the Oakland A's. Rickey considered himself the best of his time and he may have been right. The brash young outfielder was on his way to stealing 1406 bases easily exceeding the previous Major League record of 938 held by Hall of Fame outfielder Lou Brock. In one season, Rickey stole a record 130 bases.

With a relatively calm period in Washington and throughout the country, baseball prospered. Highlights of the eighties included the 1980 Philadelphia Phillies "Wheeze kids" winning the NL pennant, with a core of aging veterans that included Pete Rose, Mike Schmidt and Steve Carlton. The 1984 Detroit Tigers began the season with 35 wins against only 5 losses on their way to the AL pennant. In 1985 Rose broke Ty Cobb's all-time hit record when he got hit number 4,192. There was a great dramatic moment in the 1988 World Series when Dodger outfielder Kirk Gibson hobbled up to the plate as a pinch hitter with 2 outs and a man on in the 9th inning of game one with the Dodgers trailing by a run to the Oakland A's. Gibson was not expected to play in the series due to a serious leg injury. The Dodger fans rose as one as he made his way to home plate.

With a mighty swing of the bat he hit a ball over the left field fence to win the game. The crowd was hysterical as he hobbled around the bases. The home run propelled the Dodgers to a sweep of the A's to win the World Series. Unfortunately, Gibson was too injured to play in any of the remaining three games.

The Jim Abbott Story

A pitching phenomenon joined the California Angels in 1989. He is not in the Hall of Fame nor considered a great star but his story is one for the books. Jim Abbott pitched with only one hand. Jim was born with only one hand but with an over abundance of passion for wanting to play baseball. His high school achievements earned him a baseball scholarship to the University of Michigan where he was named the Big Ten Athlete of the year in 1988. His #31 jersey was retired by the university and he is a member of the College Baseball Hall of Fame. He was drafted by the California Angels and joined the Major League club with no minor league experience in 1989. That first year he won 12 games with an era of 3.92. In 1991, he won 18 games with an era of 2.89. and was third in balloting for the American League Cy Young Award. In 1992, his era dropped to 2.77 and in 1993 he pitched a no hitter for the New York Yankees against the Cleveland Indians. His career lasted ten years in which he won 87 games for four different teams. So, how

Jim Abbott pitching at a Calgary Cannons Minor League baseball game.

does a pitcher with only one hand play his position?

As a left hander Abbott would rest his glove on the end of his right arm in order to throw. After he released the pitch he would quickly slip his hand into the glove and be prepared to field his position. If the ball was hit to him he would place the glove with the ball under his right arm, take the ball from the glove with his left hand in time to throw the runner out at first or could even turn to throw to second to start a double play. Teams would try to bunt on him but it proved unsuccessful as he could get to the ball in time while making the switch to make the throw to first.

When playing in the American league, he was spared from batting due to the DH rule however he ended his career in the National league with the Milwaukee Brewers and went 2 for 21 as a hitter. One time he hit a triple.

In 2012, Jim Abbott wrote an autobiography, *Imperfect: An Improbable Life.*

Damage from the Lorna Prieta Earthquake, Emeryville, CA (October 17, 1989) Author: Flickr photographer sanbeiji/Joe Lewis.

Events That Shook America...

In 1989, the San Francisco took on the A's in a Series that almost wasn't. As the fans were settling in for Game 1, a 6.9 earthquake shook San Francisco and Candlestick Park. Fans were told to leave the stadium for fear of a total collapse. The city suffered massive destruction and the Series was postponed for ten days. The A's four-game sweep of the Giants became a secondary event.

The economy continued its resurgence. American consumers enjoyed a big plus in buying capabilities. This was the era of the tremendous growth of a small town discount store that was started in Bentonville, Arkansas, into a national phenomenon. Sam Walton's Walmart discount stores were popping up in almost every small community in the USA and later into the major cities. It changed the way American shopped. In technology, the PC was showing up in homes and Steve Jobs of Apple Computers and Bill Gates of Microsoft were developing computer technology and software at a rate not believed possible. Consumer markets were changing with a glut of imported products. Japanese televisions, cameras, sound systems and video games were outselling their American competition. Having evolved well past Pac-Man, video games were becoming a source of entertainment throughout American homes.

President Reagan was able to use his communications skills by improving the dialogue with Russian leader Mikhail Gorbachev that led to an easing of tensions between the two countries. This made possible the beginning of the end of the Cold War. Vice President George H.W. Bush succeeded Reagan as President in 1989. President Bush had the privilege of being president when the Berlin Wall that divided East and West Germany fell in 1989. This eventually led to the Eastern European States of the Soviet Union moving away from totalitarian rule and gaining their independence.

The Pine Tar Incident

George Brett's pine-tar bat

In the late seventies through the early eighties a bitter post season rivalry developed between the New York Yankees and the Kansas City Royals. Starting in 1976, the two teams met in four of the next five American League Championship Series with the Yanks winning three of them. The Royals couldn't stand the fiery Yankee manager Billy Martin or flamboyant owner, George Steinbrenner. In 1976, the Yanks won a highly contested five game series, 3 games to 2, after a ninth inning game 5 walk off homerun by first baseman Chris Chambliss. In 1977, the Yanks won again 3 games to 2. In 1978, it was again the Yanks, 3 games to 1. Finally the Royals broke the jinx by soundly sweeping the Yankees 3 games to 0 in 1980.

The rivalry extended into the regular seasons and on July 24, 1983 the two teams squared off at Yankee Stadium. With the Yankees leading 4-3 in the ninth and needing only one out, Kansas City's All Star third baseman George Brett came to bat with a runner on first. He carried with him one of the messy bats he had used all season. The bat was messy because of the generous amount of pine tar that Brett liked to apply to the bat handle to prevent it from slipping from his hands. Yanks manager, Billy Martin, brought in his future Hall of Fame relief pitcher Rich Gossage to get the final out. Brett turned on the second pitch and blasted it over the right field fence to gain a 5 to 4 lead. This is when it got interesting. The Yanks manager, Billy Martin, ran out to home plate and pleaded with the umpire to take a look at the bat, citing an obscure rule that pine tar cannot extend more than 18 inches from its handle. The umpire laid the bat across the 17 inch wide home plate and it was quite apparent that Martin was right. The clever Billy Martin admitted later that he had been aware of Brett's pine tar violation for some time but was waiting for the most ideal time to call attention to it. The umpires met and after consultation ruled Brett out erasing the homerun. Brett flew into a rage and ran out of his dugout out of control. The umpire had to grab him and put him in a headlock to try to control him until two Royal players came to his rescue and held him back. Meanwhile Royals pitcher Gaylord Perry ran out and grabbed the bat and started to hand it off to other teammates like a relay baton in order to hide the evidence. Two security guards got hold of the bat before it got to the locker room.

The Royals protested the game. American League President Lee McPhail, Jr. reversed the call after a lengthy study of rules and declared that the correct interpretation should have required the removal of the bat and in no way did pine tar affect the flight of the ball. The teams were forced to resume the game at Yankee stadium on August 18 at the point when Brett hit the home run. The Royals had to make a special trip to New York to play the rest of the game. It took 9 minutes to record the final 4 outs of the resumed game. The Royals were the winners 5 to 4.

Great Achievements and Americans of the Decade

1981 President Reagan shot and wounded by John Hinkley who was attempting to gain the attention of actress Jodie Foster. Sandra Day O'Connor is named first female Justice to the United States Supreme Court.

1982 The Vietnam Veterans War Memorial Wall is dedicated. Princess Grace of Monaco (formerly actress Grace Kelly) dies in car crash. First artificial heart transplant.

1983 Astronaut Sally Ride becomes first woman in space.

1985 Remains of the HMS Titanic discovered.

1988 George H.W. Bush elected as President

1989 Berlin Wall dismantled

1989 San Francisco earthquake

Cultural changes

The rise of Yuppies (Young Urban Professionals), Microsoft captures software market, CDs replace tapes and VCRs, cell phones become available.

Popular Movies, Music and Fashions

At the movies; *The Empire Strikes Back, Raiders of the lost Ark, Ferris Bueller's Day Off, Back to the Future, Ghostbusters*

Pop artists: Michael Jackson, Phil Collins, Chicago, Cyndi Lauper, Madonna, Olivia Newton John, Whitney Houston, Blondie

Fashions: Parachute pants, huge earrings, track suits, heavy metal look, Converse All-Star sneakers

FROM TOP: Sandra Day O'Connor, Michael Jackson, parachute pants, wreckage of the RMS Titanic

Baseball Milestones

1981 Player strike cancels 706 games

1982 37-year-old Steve Carlton wins record fourth Cy Young Award.

1983 Pine Tar incident

1986 Commissioner Peter Ueberroth suspend eight major league players for drug use.

1987 Reggie Jackson retires

1988 Chicago city council approves lights to be installed at Wrigley Field

1989 Commissioner Bart Giamatti bans Pete Rose from all baseball activities. San Francisco pitcher Dave Dravecky snaps arm on first pitch in comeback attempt. Commissioner Giamatti dies from a heart attack.

Trivia Quiz III 1960 – 1990

1. Who said "It's like deja vu all over"?
   a. Casey Stengel
   b. Roger Maris
   c. Yogi Berra
   d. Denny McClain

2. The M&M boys hit a total of...
   a. 120 home runs.
   b. 114 homer uns.
   c. 97 home runs.
   d. 132 home runs.

3. Name the last pitcher to win 30 games in a single season.
   a. Sandy Koufax
   b. Denny McClain
   c. Bob Gibson
   d. Steve Carlton

4. The Red Sox beat what team to win the 1967 American League pennant?
   a. Twins
   b. Tigers
   c. White Sox
   d. Yankees

5. What pitcher challenged free agency in 1973 and signed a contract with the Atlanta Braves?
   a. Andy Messersmith
   b. Bob Gibson
   c. Marvin Miller
   d. Dave McNally

6. Roberto Clemente died in a plane crash while delivering aid to what country?
   a. Ecuador
   b. Costa Rica
   c. Honduras
   d. Nicaragua

7. What batter hit .390 in 1980?
   a. Reggie Jackson
   b. George Brett
   c. Rod Carew
   d. Mike Schmidt

8. George Steinbrenner purchased the Yankees in 1983 for...
    a. $10 million.
    b. $1 billion.
    c. $100 million.
    d. $3.5 million.

9. Who won the longest professional baseball game?
    a. Chicago White Sox
    b. Rochester Red Wings
    c. Pawtucket Red Sox
    d. York White Roses

10. What commissioner banned Pete Rose from baseball?
    a. Bowie Kuhn
    b. Fay Vincent
    c. Bart Giamatti
    d. Peter Ueberroth

11. What injured LA Dodger hit a ninth inning walk off homerun in the 1988 World Series?
    a. Maury Wills
    b. Ron Fairly
    c. Willie Davis
    d. Kirk Gibson

12. Name the Yankee manager who initiated the pine tar incident.
    a. Sparky Anderson
    b. Whitey Herzog
    c. Yogi Berra
    d. Billy Martin

The Braves Take Charge

The year 1991 marked the beginning of USA military intervention in the Middle East that is still going on thirty years later. President Bush made the decision to rescue the country of Kuwait from a takeover attempt by neighboring Iraq and its dictator Sadam Hussein. The result was a 40-day intensive combat campaign called Operation Desert Storm. The American forces and allies were victorious in the first phase of the Gulf War.

The 1991 baseball season became the season of worse to first for both teams in the World Series. The Atlanta Braves and the Minnesota Twins had each come from the bottom of their league the year before. The Twins won in an extremely close seven-game World Series. The last game featured one of the great pitching duels in World Series history as Braves pitcher John Smoltz matched Jack Morris of the Twins 0-0 for 9 innings before a 10th inning pinch hit by Gene Larkin of the Twins knocked in the game winning run to win the World Series. For the Braves, 1991 marked the start of fourteen consecutive division or pennant winning seasons. This amazing streak was primarily accomplished through the pitching of three Hall of Famers, John Smoltz, Tom Glavine and Greg Maddox.

John Smoltz

Tom Glavine
Credit: Jim Accordino

Greg Maddox
Credit: Scott R. Anselmo

A Pleasant Surprise

(Courtesy of Baseball Almanac)

In 1992, Mike Piazza made his debut with the Los Angeles Dodgers. Catcher Piazza went on to an illustrious career with the Dodgers and the Mets. He is considered by many as the greatest hitting catcher of all times. His .308 career lifetime batting average was supported by 427 homeruns and 1,335 RBIs being named to 12 All Star games. Mike was elected to the Hall of Fame in 2016, but his career did not start as well as it finished.

Once a year team owners, presidents, scouts and managers get together to select whom they consider the best amateur baseball players. The order of choice is given by the past year standings, so the last place

(Continued to page 110)

Great Pitching Staffs

The Maddux, Glavine and Smoltz trio stand out as arguably the most potent team threesome of all times. Just look at these statistics and achievements accomplished during their ten years together with the Braves. Every year they won either pennants, division championships or World Series (1995).

> 468 wins (Maddux 184, Glavine 178, Smoltz 106)
> Saves 110 (all Smoltz including record breaking 55 in 2002)
> 5 Cy Young Awards (Maddux 1993,94, 95; Glavine 1998; Smoltz 1996)
> 4898 strikeouts (Maddux 1827, Glavine 1492, Smoltz 1570)
> All three are in the Hall of Fame.

That is not to slight the other great pitching staffs of the modern era.

Going back to the thirties there were brothers Dizzy and Daffy Dean who led the "Gashouse Gang" Cardinals to the 1934 World series. In two seasons (1934 and 35) the two of them combined for 96 wins and 705 strikeouts. Dizzy won an MVP and was inducted into the Hall of Fame. Paul had a short career due to injuries.

Dizzy Dean   Paul Dean

In the late forties a young Warren Spahn teamed up with Johnny Sain for the Boston Braves. Their efforts inspired a poem by Gera ld Hern of the Boston Post, "Spahn and Sain and Pray For Rain." From 1946 thru 1948 this amazing duo won 109 wins and struck out 702 batters. Sain won over twenty games in each of those three seasons. They led the Braves to the National League pennant in 1948.

First we'll use Spahn, then we'll use Sain,
Then an off day, followed by rain.
Back will come Spahn, followed by Sain,
Followed, we hope, by two days of rain.

The reason behind the New York Yankees' dominance in winning four World Series and five pennants between 1950 and 1955 was centered around four great pitchers. Allie Reynolds. Eddie Lopat, Vic Raschi and a young Whitey Ford pitched together for six seasons in which they won a total of 278 wins and 1836 strikeouts.   Ford is the only one of the four inducted into the Hall of Fame.

| Allie Reynolds | Vic Raschi | Eddie Lopat | Whitey Ford |

The 1954 Cleveland Indians won a record-setting 110 games behind Early Wynn, Bob Lemon and Mike Garcia. Their fourth starter, "Rapid" Bob Feller, also made a contribution although by then he was facing the end of his career. The combination of Wynn, Garcia and Lemon posted 65 wins (Lemon and Wynn each had 23), 294 strikeouts, and had a combined era of 2.69. Lemon and Feller are in the Hall of Fame.

  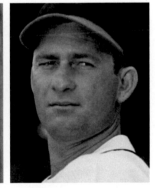

| Mike Garcia | Early Wynn | Bob Lemon |

The most dynamic tandem in the annals of baseball was possibly the five-year stretch from 1962 through 1966 enjoyed by Sandy Koufax and Don Drysdale of the Dodgers. These two were practically unbeatable. From 1962 through 1966 they won a combined 209 wins with 2551 strikeouts, and a combined era of 2.37. Between the two of them they won four Cy Young awards in five years (Drysdale 1962, Koufax 1963, 1965 and 1966). Koufax threw four no hitters. Both are in the Hall of Fame.

A Pleasant Surprise
(continued from page 107)

team picks first. In most years the players who are projected to be potential major leaguers are selected within the first three or four rounds. Players chosen towards the end of the draft are definitely not chosen for their potential for the big leagues but as fill ins for the minor league teams. Mike was chosen in the 62nd round, #1,390 of the Major League annual amateur draft.

Mike Piazza was the exception. His name was not on any team's wish list, but Mike had a connection. His father Vince was very good friends with Tommy Lasorda, the manager of the Los Angeles Dodgers. They had grown up together and Vince was the godfather to Lasorda's oldest son. As a favor to friend Vince, Lasorda talked his colleagues into drafting Mike last since it was certainly not a pick they were counting on. What a surprise it turned out to be.

New President Faces New Problems

Bill Clinton, Governor of Arkansas, succeeded George H.W. Bush as President in 1992. President Clinton, known for his energy and engaging personality, would need every bit of his charm to oversee a nation that was witnessing the growing threats of disenchantment and terrorism. He was greeted by street riots in Los Angeles when four white policemen, who had mistakenly pulled an innocent African American truck driver named Rodney King from his truck and savagely beat him, were acquitted. The reaction to the verdict turned the Watts area of LA into a scene of overturned cars, burned buildings and violent confrontations. It lasted for 6 days before order could be restored. 1995 brought more havoc when terrorist Timothy McVeigh detonated a bomb in a federal building in Oklahoma City that killed 168 people including 18 children who were in the ground floor day care center. In June of the same year the public watched on live television a three-hour police chase through Los Angeles of former Heisman trophy winner and All Pro running back O.J. Simpson. Simpson was wanted for questioning in the murder of his wife, Nicole, and her friend, Ron Goldman. A year later Americans were glued to their television for a week watching the trial of the decade when O.J. was acquitted. The extremely controversial verdict caused more civil unrest.

Baseball Faces an Old Problem

Baseball during the early nineties was heading towards its own train wreck. In 1994, another strike occurred when owners once again attempted to levy a salary cap. This time it was not for 13 days or six weeks as in the past. Players walked out on August 11 and did not return for the remainder of the season including the playoffs and World Series. The strike carried over into the following spring which delayed the start of the 1995 season and forced the cancellation of eighteen games resulting in a season of 144 games. The pain of this strike was felt by owners, players and the fans. Some fans called for a boycott of games causing a drop in attendance and a loss of advertising revenues. It would take something special to bring the fans back.

That special thing was the home run. In 1996, Major League batters hit 4962 home runs, at the time a record. There were 17 hitters with over 40 home runs lead by Oakland A's outfielder Mark McGuire with 52. This was the beginning of the home run binge that would later become identified as the Steroid Era.

Despite the home run increase there were some great pitchers in the nineties. In addition to Cy Young and future Hall of Fame pitchers of the Braves, other pitchers were striking out the home

FROM TOP: Sammy Sosa, Cal Ripken, Jr. and Mark McGuire

run bombers at a record pace. Randy Johnson of the Arizona Diamondbacks was compared to the early pitching star with the same last name, Walter "The Train" Johnson. The Arizona ace recorded 4,875 career strikeouts. Seven-time Cy Young Award winner Roger Clemens, initially with the Red Sox in the eighties became a key to the Yankee resurgence in the nineties. The great Nolan Ryan retired in 1993 after a 27-year career at the age of 44. Ryan pitched for four teams and holds the record for career strikeouts at 5,714, in addition to throwing a mind boggling seven no hitters. After retiring, Ryan became the president and part owner of the Texas Rangers.

The New York Yankees regained their dominance in the second half of the decade. Free spending owner George Steinbrenner went all out to build a championship team. They beat the Braves in the 1995 and 1996 World Series; in 1998 they beat the Padres; 1999 they beat the Braves again; in 2000 they conquered their crosstown rival the Mets, 4 games to 1. They were led by four Hall of Famers — third baseman Wade Boggs, shortstop Derek Jeter and pitchers Roger Clemens and closer Mariano Rivera.

As America moved closer to the new century the home run barrage continued reaching its peak of excitement in 1998. Outfielder Sammy Sosa of the Cubs battled St. Louis first baseman Mark McGuire for the first to break Roger Maris' 1961 single season record of 61 homeruns. The leader changed hands numerous times in what became a friendly competition between the two players. The press coverage grew with intensity each game; however, the pressure did not seem to bother either player. The final count ended with both players eclipsing the record — McGuire with 70 to Sosa's 66. Suddenly, the discontent felt by the fans due to the 1994 strike disappeared. The same year also saw a record broken that was considered unreachable — Lou Gehrig's consecutive games played. Shortstop Cal Ripken, Jr. of the Baltimore Orioles finally took to the bench after playing in an incredible 2,633 consecutive games. Enjoying this renaissance of the game was the new commissioner of baseball, Bud Selig. Closing out the century there was one more strike but of a different nature. This time the umpires walked off their jobs in 1999, however, it proved rather futile as minor league and college umpires were hired to replace them. The Major League umpires returned in a few weeks with little gained. The Atlanta Braves continued their annual trips to post season play but could only capture the World Series trophy one time (1995) in their fourteen consecutive playoff opportunities.

The Soul of Baseball

ABOVE: Buck O'Neil

"The Soul of Baseball" was the name given to Buck O'Neil by author Joe Posanki in his book of the same name. It was deservedly given for a man who stood for all that is right in baseball for over seven decades. Due to segregation, the opportunity to play Major League Baseball was unattainable for Buck. Although he did have a splendid career for the Kansas City Monarchs in the Negro Leagues, he was too old by the time Jackie Robinson broke the color barriers in 1947 to make the big leagues as a player. He did, however, serve as the first African American coach for the Chicago Cubs in 1995. He held no bitterness at not being able to play in the majors but grateful for the chance to play in the Negro Leagues with the likes of Satchel Paige and Josh Gibbons. What made Buck "the Soul of Baseball" was what he stood for in the later part of his life. He became the story teller for the Negro Leagues and a national good will ambassador for the game itself.

In 1990, Buck led the drive for the creation of the Negro League Museum in Kansas City. He went on to serve as Chairman of the Board and gained national prominence when he was featured in a Ken Burns documentary video and book *Baseball* in 1994. His electrifying presence and optimistic outlook on life and baseball made him the face of baseball for twenty years until his death in 2006 at the age of 94. In 1996, Buck was nominated for induction into the Hall of Fame by a special committee researching Negro League players. Everyone was stunned when seventeen former Negro League players were named to the Hall, but not Buck. As the man of grace that he was he said:

"Don't shed any tears. You think about this: Here I am, the grandson of a slave. And here the whole world was excited about whether I was going into the Hall of Fame or not. We've come a long ways."

He was proud to serve as the players induction presenter for the players that were enshrined that same year. Posthumously Buck was given the nation's highest honor, The Presidential Medal of Freedom, by President George Bush in 2006.

Today, he is remembered with a single red seat amidst all the blue stadium seats behind the plate at Kauffman Stadium in Kansas City.

The Dot Com Era

The 90s witnessed the advent of the Internet. Personal computers were popping up in every household. We were learning a whole new language. It became the dot com era. Apple, Microsoft and Dell became household names. Everyone was learning to search the internet, send emails, and become acquainted with a variety of computer applications. Kids were enjoying Nintendo, the 1997 gaming console. The world became smaller due to the world wide web. The way we lived and how we communicated changed our lives. It changed the way businesses operated.

Technology also scared us. As the clock moved towards midnight December 31, 1999, the world wondered what would happen to all the computer technology that had been programed with dates coded for the current century? It was called the Y2K crisis. Would all the programs implode when the clock struck midnight and the calendar changed? A sigh of relief was heard as we clicked on our PCs to find the transition to the new century was successful. Baseball welcomed the new technology as well. Computers were used to generate baseball analytics that could be used to make decisions whether during a game time to decide what batter or pitcher to use in certain situations, or in making future projections in evaluating team rosters. The new millennium had arrived.

As They Played the Game: Bo Knows

(Courtesy of Baseball Almanac)

During the eighties and nineties TV viewers became very familiar with the NIKE ad campaign: Bo Knows. The ads featured Bo Jackson, who was the 1984 Heisman Trophy winner from Auburn, an All Pro running back for the Oakland Raiders and an All-Star outfielder for the Kansas City Royals. Some thought of him as the greatest athlete of all time.

Bo was the #1 pick in the 1986 NFL draft by the Tampa Bay Buccaneers. Largely because of a bad experience with the Bucs in their recruiting approach, Bo turned down the offer and instead accepted a contract to play baseball for the Kansas City Royals with the understanding he be allowed to also play football. One year later he reentered the NFL draft where he was selected and signed by the Oakland Raiders.

Bo became the first professional baseball and football player since Jim Thorpe. Although his career in these sports was shortened by injuries, he became legendary. Royals second baseman Frank White might have said it best, "I really did play baseball with Superman." He had power, speed and athleticism beyond description. In 1989, as a Kansas City Royal, Bo hit 32 home runs with 105 RBIS. In one game, he hit four consecutive homeruns, the first three traveled over 475 feet. He hit the longest homerun on record at the time for the Royals. He was known for fielding plays that were beyond comprehension. He caught a fly ball off the wall in left field bare handed, turned and threw the runner out at home plate. Another fantastic play had him catch a fly ball in the grandstand corner in left field and throw the ball in the air to first base to double off the runner who was trying to get back to first after the catch. His strength was unmatched. He would break a bat over his thigh in frustration with being struck out. Negro League All Star Buck O'Neil said when he heard the sound of the crack of the bat after Bo would hit, it reminded him of two players, Babe Ruth, and Josh Gibson, the all-time Negro league home run hitter. A hip injury ended Bo's all pro football career in 1991. Despite a hip replacement surgery, Bo remained in baseball until 1994. His legendary two-sport career is still discussed 25 years later.

News of the Era

1990 Mafia boss John Gotto arrested and sentenced to life imprisonment for murder, racketeering and other crimes

1991 Persian Gulf War erupts: Arkansas Governor Bill Clinton elected President: Los Angeles race riots

1993 Hubble telescope launched into space providing research photographs of the universe. Waco, Texas 51-day Branch Davidian headquarter siege tragedy, 76 people died. The North American Trade Agreement is signed (NAFTA). Basketball star Michael Jordan makes unsuccessful attempt to play major league baseball for the Chicago White Sox.

1994 Jackie Onassis dies: Olympic Ice Skater Nancy Kerrigan suffers broken knee in an attack by friends of competitor Tonya Harding attempting to prevent her from participating in the Olympic games.

1996 Golfer Tiger Woods wins his first Masters championship at the age of 21. Atlanta Olympics Games are tarnished by terrorist Eric Rudolph who denonates a bomb that resulted in 2 deaths and 111 injured bystanders.

1997 Mother Teresa dies; Princess Diana dies in car accident in Paris; Author J.K. Rowling introduces Harry Potter in the United Kingdom

1998 Senator and astronaut John Glenn returns to space in Space Shuttle at the age of 77.

1999 Columbine school tragic shooting killing 12 students and 1 teacher

TOP LEFT: Inauguration of President Bill Clinton (1992)
ABOVE: The Hubble Space Telescope and Tiger Woods

Baseball Happenings

1991 Atlanta Braves outfielder Deion Sanders enters agreement to play football for the Oakland Raiders.

1993 Nolan Ryan retires with 5714 career strikeouts and seven no hitters

1995 Mickey Mantle dies from liver cancer at the age of 63.

1997 Seattle sets all-time team homeruns in a single season 264.

1998 Cal Ripken Jr. retires with a record of 2632 consecutive games played. New York Yankees win record breaking 114 games.

1999 Yankee great Joe Dimaggio dies.

Popular Movies, Music and Fashions

Popular movies: *Jurassic Park, Forest Gump, Toy Story, Titanic, Schindlers List*

Pop Music Stars: Britney Spears, Nirvana, Sheryl Crowe, Bono, Madonna

Fashions: Grunge look, fluorescent clothing, hoop earrings, hush puppies

Books: Harry Potter, Angela Ashes, Stephen King, John Grisham

Vin Turns Off His Mic

Vin Scully
Credit: Floatjon

On October 2, 2016, longtime Dodger broadcaster Vin Scully shut down his microphone and retired at the age of 88. Vin was the most admired broadcaster of his time. His style was simple and consistent. He was taught not to be a "homer" by his mentor, the famous Red Barber, when he joined the Dodgers in 1952. Consequently, he did not show his allegiance to the Dodgers, only to the game itself. When the big hit occurred, Vin would turn the mic towards the crowd to let the listeners feel the excitement rather than feature his talking over the event. Vin was with the Dodgers for 65 of his 67-year career. He called

(Continued to page 116)

11

Another New Century

George W. Bush was inaugurated in 2001 just nine months before the 9/11 terrorist attack by the Islamic extremist group Al Qaeda under the direction of its leader Osama Bin Laden. The horrors of over 3,000 U.S. citizens killed in the World Trade Center, the Pentagon, and the airliner crash in Pennsylvania marked the beginning of a presidency filled with difficulties and tough decisions. On March 20, 2003, the USA initiated an invasion of Iraq under the false impression that Iraq's dictator, Saddam Hussein, had accumulated and planned to use weapons of mass destruction against the USA. America's 130,000 troops, along with 30,000 allied troops, invaded Iraq with full force for 40 days before Bush declared the mission accomplished on May 1. History has shown he was very premature in his declaration as the war continued for eight years and witnessed the creation of another well-armed extremist group named ISIS. In December of 2003, Saddam Hussein was captured and was later convicted and sentenced to death as a war criminal by the new Iraq government.

First responders at the World Trade Center

Vin Turns Off His Mic (continued from page 115)

Dodger games when Jackie Robinson was playing second base. He was behind the mic for Don Larsen's perfect game in 1955, Sandy Koufax's perfect game, Hank Aaron's 715th home run, Kirk Gibson's incredible World Series home run in 1987 and so many more historical moments. He felt the pain of the Dodgers leaving Brooklyn for LA in 1957. His soft voice and gentlemanly manners were a fixture in millions of homes through the good and bad times of our country's history for more than a half of century. He was awarded every kind of honor a broadcaster could achieve. These included the Ford C. Frick Award from the Hall of Fame (1982) and Presidential Medal of Freedom (2016), and a star on the famous Hollywood Walk of Fame.

The emotions ran high when Vin signed off for his last game with a final wish and prayer: "I have said enough for a lifetime and, for the last time, I wish you all a very pleasant good afternoon," he said. "There will be a new day, and eventually a new year, and when the upcoming winter gives way to spring, ah, rest assured, once again, it will be time for Dodgers baseball. So this is Vin Scully wishing you a very pleasant good afternoon, wherever you may be."

In ranking the greatest broadcasters of all time, Dan Levy of Bleacher Reports spoke for millions of baseball fans, "Scully was simply the best."

Baseball has, since its inception, offered a healing console to our country's pains. Twenty days following the tragedy of 9/11, baseball returned to New York City. To a sellout crowd and national TV audience, the New York Mets hosted the Atlanta Braves in what was an emotional start to the healing process for the country. A patriotic salute to the first responders and victims of the tragedy allowed the nation to cry together and collectively feel the relief that the call of "Play Ball" can bring. When the Mets' Mike Piazza hit a two-run homer in the eighth inning to take the lead, the cheers of the crowd were a sign that America was starting a return to normalcy.

Steroids

The 2001 season was a memorable season for baseball. San Francisco outfielder Barry Bonds broke the McGuire home run record when he hit 73. In the American League, Alex Rodriguez (A-Rod) who had signed a $250 million, 10-year contract with the Texas Rangers, was connecting almost as much as Bonds. Others were showing an amazing increase in power which was causing some to wonder "Why?" Accusations made were eventually confirmed that many players were injecting themselves with illegal steroids to gain strength and overcome injuries. Investigations included a 2005 Congressional Hearing questioning three well-known ballplayers: Sammy Sosa, Mark McGuire, and Rafael Palmeiro of the Orioles. The following year Barry Bonds was at the center of a Senate Investigation Committee for illegal use of performance-enhancing drugs. In 2010, pitcher Roger Clemens of the Yankees was called to testify before Congress. Although no players were convicted in a court of law, many including A-Rod, then with the Yankees, received 60 game suspensions. Many reputations, including that of Barry Bonds, were tarnished, as were their individual records. The incidents placed a dark cloud over Major League Baseball and became known as the Steroid Era.

Outside of baseball, more bad news haunted the country. In 2005, Americans were stunned watching the videos of the viciousness of Hurricane Katrina as it struck New Orleans leaving a death

A water tower in Louisiana collapses during Hurricane Katrina.

toll of over 2,000 and many thousands of displaced residents. In 2007, a lone gunman killed 32 and injured 17 students on the campus of Virginia Tech University. In the beginning of 2006, there were signs of a troubled economy. These signs mushroomed into a full-scale recession by 2008 caused primarily by banks issuing sub-prime mortgages to those who would not have ordinarily qualified for home ownership. Because the mortgages were issued with no down payment on over-inflated housing values, millions of homeowners were unable to make their mortgage payments. This caused the stock market and housing values to tumble while unemployment rates surged to over 10 percent. Anxiety ruled the nation as doomsayers predicted a repeat of the 1929 depression. The government was forced in the position of bailing out some of the nation's largest lending institutions and car manufacturers. The recession eventually began a slow recovery in 2010 but not before millions of people suffered financial hardships.

On the field, the turn of the century had its share of excitement. 2001 welcomed two future Hall of Famers. Twenty-seven-year-old rookie Ichiro Suzuki was lured from Japan with a three-year 14-million-dollar contract. In his first year in the major leagues, Ichiro led the Seattle Mariners to a record-setting 116 wins with his .350 batting average, 56 stolen bases and 242 hits. He was the first player since Jackie Robinson to lead the league in both batting average and stolen bases. He was named the 2001 MVP and Rookie of the Year. The achievements just kept coming; 10-time All-Star, 10-time gold glove winner, seven-time hits leader to name a few. In 2004, he collected 262 hits to break Hall of Famer George Sisler's 84-year-old record for most hits in a season. Ichiro returned to the Mariners after three-year stints with the Yankees and the Marlins and retired in 2018. His 3,089 Major League hits are the most ever by a foreign player. If combined with the 1,278 hits accumulated while playing for the Japanese Orix Bluewave, Ichiro's total number of career hits – 4,367 – surpasses Pete Rose's Major League record of 4,256.

The other phenom that season was Albert Pujols, first baseman of the St Louis Cardinals. The 21-year-old Dominican Republic native won the NL Rookie of the Year Award batting .329 with 37 home runs and a league-leading 130 RBIs. In his eleven years with the Cardinals, he was named MVP three times, played in nine All-Star Games and led the team to three NL pennants and two World Series Championships. In his 2004 MVP season, he batted .359 with 43 home runs and 124 RBIs. The Los Angeles Angels outbid all others when Albert became a free agent after the 2011 season with a 100-million-dollar contract. Through 17 seasons he has accumulated over 3,000 hits with more than 600 home runs and is a sure bet to enter the Hall of Fame after he retires.

Ichiro Suzuki/Credit: Barbara Moore

Albert Pujols/Credit: Keith Allison

In 2004, on the 100th anniversary of World Series championships, the Boston Red Sox broke the "Curse of Bambino" when they won the World Series in a four-game sweep of the St Louis Cardinals. It was the first Red Sox championship since 1923 – the year they traded Ruth to the Yankees. They did it the hard way having gotten into the playoffs as a wild card team by finishing second to the Yankees. They were able to defeat the Anaheim Angels to earn the right to play for the AL pennant. However, they lost the first three games of the seven-game series of the pennant series against the Yanks. No wild card team had previously come back from a three-game deficit in the playoffs to win the pennant until the Boston Red Sox did that season. Amazingly they continued their hot streak by defeating the Cardinals four straight to win the World Series. The series was highlighted by a display of courage by Red Sox pitcher Curt Shilling who pitched with an injured ankle that was bleeding through his sock. Theo Epstein was the General Manager of the Sox and was lauded for his skill in assembling this championship team.

The year 2005 saw the end of the Braves 14 consecutive division championships. In 2007, Barry Bonds broke Hank Aaron's home run record and retired with 762 home runs. Baseball established an annual tribute game day to the civil rights movement and Jackie Robinson in 2008. Each season since then all teams play one game, often in retro uniforms, with players wearing Robinson's number 42.

In national news, Barack Obama was sworn in as president in 2009. He became the first African American to hold the highest office in the country. The new president inherited the challenge of fixing the broken economy along with the ongoing search for Al Qaeda leader Osama Bin Laden. In 2012, Bin Laden was killed when a group of U.S. Navy Seals invaded the farmhouse in which he was hiding in Pakistan. The same year saw the tragic murder of 29 people including 22 students, ages 5-7, by a crazed shooter at Sandy Hook Elementary School in Sandy Hook, Connecticut. Terrorism hit America again in 2013 when two brothers under the influence of ISIS set off two bombs near the finish line of the Boston Marathon. Three people died, sixteen lost limbs, and over one hundred others were injured. One of the brothers died, and the other was captured and sentenced to life in prison. Once again, baseball played a part in the healing process as Boston Red Sox star first baseman David "Big Papi" Ortiz presented on national TV an emotional challenge at Fenway Park for Boston to stand strong.

David Ortiz (Courtesy of Baseball Almanac)

The 2010s

The second decade in baseball of the new millennium started with a back and forth 2011 seven-game World Series between the Cardinals and the Texas Rangers.   The Cardinals won in seven but only after a slugfest Game 6 that saw the lead change 6 times until the Cardinals won 10 to 9. In that game, the Rangers came within one pitch of winning the championship. They were leading 7-5 in the bottom of the ninth with 2 outs and 2 strikes on batter third baseman David Freese. Freese ruined the moment with a two-run homer to force the game into extra innings. Undeterred Ranger outfielder Josh Hamilton smashed a 10th inning to take back the lead. Not for long. Cardinal first baseman Lance Berkman responded with a home run in the bottom of 10th sending the game into the 11th. The Rangers failed to score in the top of the 11th setting the stage for the 9th inning hero David Freese. David did not disappoint. After being greeted with standing ovation by the hometown Cardinal fans, he hammered a game-winning walk-off home run. It is not difficult to find a Cardinal fan who can recite the details of that game many years later.

The Houston Astros moved from the National League to the American League in 2013 to balance out each league with 15 teams and three divisions consisting of 5 teams. 2016 brought the long-suffering Chicago fans their reward, when the Cubbies outlasted the Cleveland Indians to win their first World Series since 1908, 4 games to 3. It was a sleepy country the morning following Game 7. After a rain delay, the game lasted into the morning hours before outfielder Ben Zobrist delivered a game-winning double in the tenth inning for an 8-7 victory! The turnout for the jubilant Chicago celebration parade two days later was estimated at five million people. The general manager of the Cubs was non-other than Theo Epstein who had put together the 2004 Red Sox when they ended their World Series drought. He accomplished this championship by strictly sticking to a rebuilding program he implemented when he joined the Cubs in 2011. The excitement in Chicago rippled throughout the country. Baseball once again exhibited its galvanizing impact on bringing people together. We have often witnessed how the spirit of baseball has engaged our cities with excitement and pride as their team drives towards winning the championship. Baseball has enabled Americans to put aside their disagreements and come together to support their team.

The 2010s witnessed a tremendous youth movement in baseball. Teams began to rely on the athleticism of players under the age of 25. Partly because of the tremendous savings of playing young ballplayers before they became unrestricted free agents. However, by 2015 when the small market Kansas City Royals won the World Series with their young players, it was obvious the strategy could pay off with a championship team. This was followed in 2016 when the youthful Chicago Cubs broke their 108-year-old World Series drought. The Houston Astros continued to show the youthful rebuild approach worked in 2017 when they were victorious over the heavily favored, high payroll team the Los Angeles Dodgers.

Another change of this era was the advent of the six-inning starting pitcher. Teams began relying on a pitching specialist to pitch the seventh inning and a specialist for the eighth inning in addition to the traditional ninth-inning closer role. This allowed the starting pitchers to throw fewer innings. Complete games thrown by a starting pitcher were rare — only 2.4% in 2016. That compares to over 50% in earlier eras.

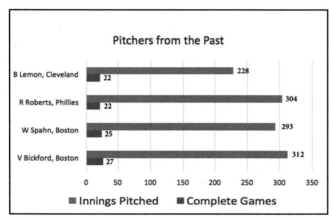

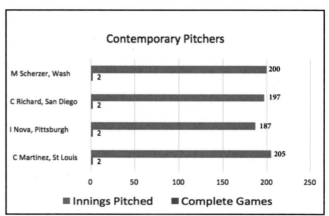

Along with pitching, hitting was taking on a different look. Striking out, which was at one time considered an unforgivable sin, has now become acceptable if it means a batter will hit more home runs. Batters are swinging for the fences by turning to an upward swing as opposed to a level swing. More hits and more home runs at the cost of increased strikeouts. It is entirely possible that there will be seasons in which there will be more strikeouts than hits. Striking out 25% of bats is common. A giant leap from the days of DiMaggio, Ted Williams, Tony Gwynn or George Brett who would put the ball in play 90% of times.

Baseball continued to welcome more young stars as the decade moved on. The Yankees 20-year-old outfielder Aaron Judge won the AL Rookie of the Year award in 2017 by hitting 52 home runs. 24-year-old Jose Altuve of the Astros won the MVP of the NL in 2017 by batting .346 and scoring 112 runs. He was also named the 2017 Sportsman of the Year by *Sports Illustrated* magazine. Mike Trout, only 26, of the Angels has been cited as the face of baseball due to his .306 batting average, 201 HRs, 569 RBIs and 165 stolen bases in his first six seasons. He has been named to the All-Star game roster every year he has played, has won two MVP awards, and was named Rookie of the Year in 2012. Mike has also enhanced his appeal due to his All-American character off the field. Giancarlo Stanton was traded from the Marlins to the Yankees bringing with him his 59 home runs from 2017 to complement Aaron Judge's outstanding power display.

Other young players making their debut in 2018 were pitcher/outfielder Shohei Ohtani of the Los Angeles Angels (the first player since Babe Ruth to play as both a pitcher and batter), 20-year-old outfielder Ronald Acuna Jr. of the Atlanta Braves and 20-year-old All Star second basemen Ozzie

Albies. Juan Soto, the youngest player in the majors at 19 years old, is roaming the outfield for the Washington Nationals. There are many more overachieving young ballplayers embarking on possible Hall of Fame type careers.

The second decade of the new century also showed a country undergoing change. Although the economy was improving American workers were not satisfied with their stagnant paychecks. Congress was straddled with divisiveness and nothing seemed to get done. Political change was in the air. In 2016 wealthy entrepreneur Donald J. Trump narrowly defeated Hillary R. Clinton, the first woman ever to run for president. It was a political campaign as never seen before in the country's history. President Trump's campaign rally cry "Make America Great Again" carried over into his presidency amidst controversy and causing even greater political division.

The environment was also very much back in the news. Three damaging hurricanes hit Texas, Florida and Puerto Rica in September and October of 2017. Massive fires hit the state of California while glaciers were disappearing in Alaska. All of which caused alarm about the seriousness of climate change and the future of the planet.

As They Played the Game

Jim Morris joined the ranks of the many highly touted high school players who failed to make it to the major leagues. Jim was drafted in the first round of the 1983 draft by the Milwaukee Brewers. After four years of struggling in the lower minor leagues and fighting off many arm and shoulder injuries, the former fastball whiz hung up his cleats and returned home in 1987 to start a new career. His chosen path was that of a high school science teacher and baseball coach in Reagan County, Texas. Jim was able to lift the high school team's run of the mill baseball team, the Big Lake Owls, to new heights and in 1998 they won the district championship. As a coach Jim spent hours pitching batting practice to his players. As he did, he felt his arm strength returning. The players urged him to give professional baseball another try, but Jim realized that at the age of 35 his career was over, or was it? The evening before the district championship game Jim playfully told the team that if they won the game he would attend a tryout camp with a major league team. They won, and Jim was forced to hold up his

(Courtesy of the Baseball Almanac)

end of the bargain.

Two months later, after many strenuous workouts, Jim showed up with a bunch of teenage kids at a try-out session for the Tampa Bay Devil Rays. The coaches were incredulous that a 35-year-old retread pitcher thought he could pitch in the major leagues. But they watched and were astonished when they witnessed his 98-mph fastball strike out the young hitters. He was signed to a contract, and after a few months back in the minors, Jim Morris made his Major League debut as a 35-year-old rookie on July 25, 1999. In his first game, he struck out Royce Clayton in the eighth inning in a game against the Texas Rangers.

Unfortunately, the dream lasted only two seasons as the recurring arm problems returned and Jim retired in 2000 after appearing in just 21 games with an era of 4.80, and no wins to his credit. He returned to Texas to resume his teaching career after reaching his dream.

In 2002, Walt Disney Company released *The Rookie*, a popular movie based on Jim's inspiring comeback.

American Happenings and Events in the New Millennium

9/11/2001 Terrorists attack the World Trade Center, Pentagon and American Airline Flight 11

2003 American and Allied forces invade Iraq

2005 Hurricane Katrina strikes New Orleans

2008 Barrack Obama elected President of the United States

2010 Massive BP oil spill in Gulf of Mexico

2016 Donald J. Trump elected President of the United States

Popular Movies, Music and Fashions

Pop Artists: Jennifer Lopez, U2, Lady Gaga, Beyonce, Jay-Z, Taylor Swift, Usher, Rihanna

Favorite Movies: *Pirates of the Carribean, Spider-Man, La La Land, Boyhood, Lincoln, Beautiful Mind*

Fashion looks: oversized jerseys, gauchos, denim skirts, Chinese slippers, puffy jackets, cornrows

Baseball Milestones

2001 Seattle Mariners set new modern-day record for most wins in a season 116 (Chicago Cubs also won 116 games in 1906). Barry Bonds breaks single season home run record with 73.

2003 Rickey Henderson retires with career records of 1,406 career stolen bases and 2295 runs scored.

2004 Mariners Ichiro Suzuki sets new single season hit record with 262 hits. Giants Barry Bonds sets record for single season walks 232

2007 Barry Bonds retires with career records of 762 home runs and 2,558 walks

2008 Francisco Rodriquez of the Los Angeles Angels sets a new single season records with 62 saves. Texas Rangers set new record with 378 doubles.

2014 Yankees Mariano Rivers retires with record for most career saves 652.

2018 Japanese pitcher/outfielder Shohei Ohtani debuts with the Los Angeles Angels

FROM TOP: A man holding a turtle covered with residue of the BP oil spill, a man dressed as Captain Jack Sparrow, Lady Gaga, and a pair of gauncho pants.

Looking Ahead

Since the Civil War, Americans have lived through the tragedy of wars, the pain of recessions and a depression, the excitement of new technology, and a continuing evolution of a changing society. Baseball has been our companion through the good and the bad. What does the future hold for this beloved pastime?

The game itself has never been better. The athletes are stronger, faster and better equipped than ever. The 2018 All Star game rosters, which in the past have been dominated by veteran ballplayers, contained 30% of players under the age of 26. Many of these players will be playing well into the 2030s. Ballpark attendance has never been higher. The newer stadiums have added attractions and concessions to keep attendees engaged and enthused throughout the game. At the ire of some old timers, Major League Baseball has done an outstanding job of adding family friendly attractions. Young fans can evaluate their skills in batting cages and pitching machines. The new scoreboards put up entertaining and informative videos. The teams have hilarious mascots that interact with the fans. Popular music is played between innings. Many have called going to the ballpark a Disney experience.

Baseball is reaching further into the international market. A separate draft has been arranged for foreign players. Team scouts now travel the world seeking the top players. A few games each year are scheduled each year in Europe and Japan. The World Baseball Classic played every four years in the spring has garnered a lot of attention. There are 16 countries represented with native major and minor league players. The teams play in front of excited audiences in different countries to earn the opportunity to play for the WBC championship.

Cracks In The Armor That Baseball Must Confront

As good as it was for the players to move out from under the reserve clause it changed the financial structure of professional baseball. Players became expensive commodities. They are not just baseball players, they are celebrities. Fans flock to the stadiums to see their favorite players which has driven up the players salary demands. The average team payroll in 2018 was $150 million. There must be enough revenue to cover the cost of these salaries in addition to all of the added attractions at the ballpark. Game tickets and concessions can only pay so much. The rest comes from television and advertising revenue. As the cost of baseball operations goes up so does an increase in ticket prices and the number of commercials. Baseball games 40 years ago rarely extended more than 2 ½ hours. The average game now lasts over three hours to accommodate the extra marketing activities. In order to receive top advertising revenues, games must be televised in primetime. World Series games start at 8:30 p.m. eastern time. The results are that these games do not end until past midnight eastern and past 11 p.m. central time – entirely too late for kids and many working adults to watch the national pastime's greatest event. This is no way to groom future fans. Baseball historian Jacques Barzun, who quoted the subtitle to this book, "Whoever wants to know the heart and mind of America, had better learn baseball," had this to say about the contemporary era of professional baseball:

"I've gotten so disgusted with baseball, I don't follow it anymore. I just see the headlines and turn my head in shame from what we have done with our most interesting, best, and healthiest pastime. The commercialization is beyond anything that was ever thought of, the overvaluing, really, of the game itself. It's out of proportion to the place an entertainment ought to have. Other things are similarly commercialized and out of proportion, but for baseball, which is so intimately connected with the nation's spirit and tradition, it's a disaster."

Baseball Management

The escalation of salaries and multi-year player contracts has changed how team owners and general managers evaluate a player's value. Trades are made much more cautiously with the added complexity and cost of a player. As of this writing there is a team payroll cap of $190 million. If a team surpasses that amount the ownership is assessed with a heavy luxury tax penalty. The object is to prevent the larger market teams, i.e. Yankees, Dodgers, and others, from buying up all the best players. The money collected from the tax is distributed to the smaller market teams in order to keep a competitive balance in the chase for the pennants. There has always been an imbalance of resources among the teams that has favored the larger market teams. The best way for the smaller teams to compete is to field younger players who have yet to reach the free agent plateau of the multi-million dollar, multi-year contracts. Consequently, trades are often made based on the contract of the player more than the talent level. Many teams will resort to trading talented ballplayers off to other teams in order to lower payroll. They will then proceed to start a rebuild process which often takes three to five years before achieving a competitive team. The 2015 Royals, 2016 Cubs, 2017 Astros all went through this dilemma before winning their championships.

Player contracts can also affect how the team is managed on the field. Teams are very hesitant to take the chance of risking an injury to a player to whom they are paying a multi-million-dollar salary. Therefore, what were considered relatively minor injuries in the past that a player could play through, now may result in sending a player to the disabled list to protect the financial investment.

Fans are seeing more platooning than ever. In the past platooning was pretty much limited to substituting a left-handed batter for a righty, and vice versa, depending on whether the pitcher was right-handed or left-handed. Now we are seeing large scale changes in player positioning. For some right-handed batters, the second baseman may move to the left side of the infield as the batter is more likely to pull the ball to that side of the field. The same practice is used for a left-handed hitter by moving the shortstop to the right side of the infield. There are times when the defense looks like the traditional softball game tactic of playing a middle fielder.

Is the game too long? Much to the concern of Major League Baseball ball games in 2017 a nine-inning game lasted an average of 3 hours and 5 minutes, the longest on record. Young fans in particular want to see more action and less time changing pitchers, visits to the mound, batters stepping out of the batter box and pitchers taking too long between pitches. The homerun dominated and specialized pitching era teams are using more pitchers, which means extra time added to make the pitching changes. At the same time batters are being more selective and running up the ball/strike count waiting for the perfect pitch. All this adds up to longer games.

The Commissioner has instituted a number of changes aimed at speeding up the game. These include installing a pitch clock that penalizes a pitcher with an automatic called ball if the pitch is not delivered in 18 seconds after the throw back from the catcher. Another new rule is limiting the number of times coaches, players and managers can visit the mound. The counter argument to these problems is that it is the current cycle of power baseball that is causing the long games and that eventually the cycle will swing back as it has in the past to contact pitching versus strikeout pitching which will diminish the walks and allow pitchers to stay in the game longer.

There are also potential labor problems looming due to the slowdown of the signing of free agents. In 2018, over one hundred free agents were not signed when spring training camps opened, which resulted in creating a special spring training camp for these players to get in shape. This has not happened since the strike year of 1994/95. The players' union is questioning whether the owners have colluded in an attempt to bring down salaries. The owners take the position that the demands by the players' agents for longer term contracts is creating very risky investments, particularly for players over thirty years old. The onslaught of younger players maturing earlier has diminished the value of super star veterans who often pass their peak years in their early thirties.

Danger at the Ballpark

"Danger at the Ballkpark" (2017, TriMark Press) is the title of a book by Miami lawyer Jack Herskowitz, which examines the dangers awaiting the unsuspecting fan from a foul bar or flying bat while sitting in lower field seats at major and minor league stadiums. The dangers have been brought to the attention of the public due to the many near fatal incidents that have occurred in recent years. On September 21, 2017, a foul ball off the bat of Yankee third baseman Todd Frazier hit a two-year-old little girl squarely in the face causing multiple facial fractures and fears of brain damage. It was fortunate that it was not fatal as the ball was traveling at approximately 105 mph as it left the bat. Days after the incident the girl's forehead was marked by the imprint left by stitches on the ball that hit her.

Fans and players were stunned as the game was temporarily stopped while the little girl was carried up the stairs in the arms of her grandfather. The batter Frazier stated, " I thought of my kids, you know? It was terrible. I am shaken up." Frazier had dropped to one knee overcome by emotion when the incident occurred.

The result has been a much delayed response by professional baseball to expand the protective netting that has been in place behind home plate to encompass all lower field seats from well past third base to beyond first base. Some fans are concerned that it will decrease the value of seats claiming the netting intrudes upon their view. Others believe the netting should be extended even farther.

Where Are The Black Ballplayers?

Take a look at the rosters of today's Major League teams. There are very few African American players — only 8% — a decline of approximately 60% of black ballplayers from 30 years ago. Compare that to 78% of NBA players and 67% in the NFL. What is going on? Reginald Howard, a surviving player from the Negro League, has some strong opinions.

Reginald experienced the demise of the Negro League as an infielder for the Indianapolis Clowns in the 1950s. Before his time as a player he served as the bat boy for the Chicago Giants during the 1940s. Reginald saw them all play, including Satchel Paige, Josh Gibson, and Buck O'Neal. " As great as Jackie Robinson was, he was not the best. These guys could play with anyone. But once the big leagues added the star players onto their rosters the Negro League fans turned their attention to Major League baseball. "During the decades of the 1950s and 60s black players were an integral part of MLB, but now fifty years later they are scarce. So, what happened?

In his youth Reginald felt he was guided away from baseball and into track because of his speed. The speed, strength, quickness, and agility of the black athlete was more highlighted in basketball and football. A prevailing attitude among the white coaches and sports organizers was the unfounded belief that "we did not like baseball. We did not want to play baseball." This attitude consequently led to a lack of sponsorships for inner city baseball." If you can't get the five, six, seven or eight-year-old youngster involved, when he gets to nine and ten and ready to play, he is not going to want to play. How much better would baseball be today, if we had 40%, 50% or 60% of the players African American? "

So what is Major League baseball doing to recognize this problem? Certainly, a lot of talk but maybe not enough action. The recognition of Jackie Robinson with the annual Jackie Robinson Day

More efforts are needed to get black fans to the ballpark.

is a nice tribute to a great man but it is just a starting point. The Negro League Museum in Kansas City is another great idea. There has been, in recent years, more attention given to sponsoring inner city baseball but there has to be more. More efforts need to be directed at getting the black fans back to the ballpark.

It is easy to see the small representation of black fans at the games. Higher ticket prices have been an inhibitor to the lower economic minority population. Some teams have moved out of their inner-city locations to the more higher income suburbs.

In Conclusion

As we have witnessed, the environment around the games is constantly changing. Yet through wars, racial strife, labor woes and market demands, the game itself does not change. The bases remain 90 feet apart, the pitcher throws from 60 feet 6 inches, homeplate is 17 inches wide and there are nine players on the field. In the movie *Field of Dreams* there is a scene towards the end of the movie when Terrance Mann, played by James Earl Jones, encourages Ray Kinsella, played by Kevin Costner, not to give up on his dream. It is a very meaningful sentiment that shares the objective of this book of bringing baseball and history together. It also carries a lesson that our divided country should listen to today:

"The one constant through all the years, Ray, has been baseball. America has rolled by like an army of steamrollers. It has been erased like a blackboard, rebuilt and erased again. But baseball has marked the time. This field, this game: it's a part of our past, Ray. It reminds of us of all that once was good and it could be again. Oh... people will come Ray. People will most definitely come."

The baseball field in Iowa featured in the movie "Field of Dreams."

Final Comprehensive Trivia Quiz

1.   The Atlanta Braves won _____ consecutive pennants or division season winning seasons
a.   4
b.   10
c.   14
d.   8

2.   Dizzy and Paul Dean pitched for _____
a.   St Louis Cardinals
b.   Pittsburgh Pirates
c.   Philadelphia Phillies
d.   Cleveland Indians

3.   Who was called "The Soul of Baseball?
a.   Bo Jackson
b.   Jackie Robinson
c.   Buck O'Neil
d.   Babe Ruth

4.   Barry Bonds broke Roger Maris's homerun record of 61 with how many ?
a.   63
b.   74
c.   73
d.   66

5.   What team did "Big Papi" play for
a.   Yankees
b.   Orioles
c.   Dodgers
d.   Red Sox

6.   The Chicago Cubs won the World Series in 2016. How many years had passed since its last World Series Championship?
a.   90
b.   34
c.   108
d.   120

7.   What was King Kelly of the 1894 Red Sox most known for.
a.   homeruns
b.   striking out
c.   stealing bases
d.   throwing no hitters

8.   Ty Cobb won ___ consecutive batting titles.
a.   6
b.   10
c.   9
d.   12

9.   In 1941 Ted Williams batted .406 but did not win the MVP award. Who did?
a.   Stan Musial
b.   Joe Dimaggio
c.   Bob Feller
d.   Hank Greenberg

10.   Who had the nickname "Say Hey"
a.   Willie Mays
b.   Mickey Mantle
c.   Duke Snider
d.   Al Rosen

11.   Name the triple crown winner who led his team to the AL pennant in 1967
a.   Reggie Jackson
b.   Pete Rose
c.   Carl Yastrzemski
d.   Reggie Jackson

12.   How many no hitters did Nolan Ryan throw ?
a.   5
b.   3
c.   7
d.   12

13.   "Spahn and Sain and pray for rain" referred to what team?
a.   Boston Red Sox
b.   Philadelphia A's
c.   Pittsburgh Pirates
d.   Boston Braves

14. Name the last pitcher to win 30 games in a season
a. Robin Roberts
b. Christy Mathewson
c. Tom Seaver
d. Denny McClain

15. Which active player has appeared in six all star games in his first six seasons?
a. Mike Trout
b. Freddie Freeman
c. Bryce Harper
d. Jose Altuve

Answers: 1. (c), 2. (a) 3. (c) 4. (c) 5. (d) 6. (c) 7. (c) 8. (c) 9. (b) 10. (a) 11. (c) 12. (c) 13. (d) 14. (d) 15. (a)

Family Traditions

Baseball has occupied an important space with many American families. Whether at the ballpark or as background sound to summer evenings on the porch listening on the radio or watching it on television in the house. Friends gather at sports bars to play trivia while others are engrossed in playing fantasy baseball.

There is the joy of a summer evening watching or coaching the kids in Little League. It is as American as apple pie. Playing catch in the backyard with the kids or playing as an adult on your church or company softball team, it becomes an important ingredient in your life. Family trips, sometimes hundreds of miles, are taken to watch their favorite team. Many will make an annual pilgrimage to Florida or Arizona to watch spring training games. It is part of us and our heritage.

The following are four fan and family stories. If you have one send it to jwhalloran@aol.com If there are enough they may be made into a book.

Enjoy the stories and enjoy baseball.

Mike Nabors with his dad, Bob.

Two Idols

As I make the turn around third and head towards another trip towards home at the ripe "young" age of 50, it's amazing how baseball has dominated my life. I place the blame solely on my father whose passion for the game was surely passed on to me.

My father grew up in Tampa, which may not have had a big league team at the time, but it was the Major League mecca for spring training. His tales of getting autographs from the likes of Enos Slaughter, Stan Musial and his favorite, Jackie Robinson, made a big impact on me. My Dad loved and appreciated Robinson and because of this made the Brooklyn Dodgers his team. I learned at an early age the price Robinson paid to break the color barrier through my Dad's stories.

Baseball was more than a sport, it was a history lesson.

When I was nine years old, my Dad introduced me to the game courtesy of Houston's Class A affiliate, those Cocoa Astros. The year was 1977 where our first game together saw minor league baseball offer a few guarantees each night – always a good seat and more than your fair share at a few foul balls.

On that Cocoa Astros team there were many more talented, many more athletic players, but for our money, Bruce Bochy was mine and my Dad's favorite player. The Cocoa catcher was easily the slowest player on the team and in his full season there hit a modest .253 with three homers and 35 RBI in 128 games, but we didn't care about his stats.

We liked Bochy because he liked me. He would always sign autographs but gave us much more, his time. He asked about my little league team and treated me with respect.

Amazingly, 41 years later Bruce Bochy is a future Hall of Fame Manager with the San Francisco Giants. Almost as amazing was that Bochy made it to the Major Leagues the year after we cheered him on in Cocoa. My Dad and I even just happened to see Bochy's first Major League home run in the Astrodome. A remarkable run.

Dad and I have been to World Series games, All Star contests, enjoyed seeing Wrigley and Fenway together and have traveled all around the country in search of nearly every big league stadium, yet for my money nothing will top watching Bochy and the Class A Astros. It was my first taste of the game, a game that has been great to so many and formed a bond between me and my father.

I learned at an extremely early age that I loved baseball but didn't have anything close to the ability to be a professional so I chose the next best path, a career in the media. I've been a sports broadcast journalist for over 25 years where I always got a kick out of periodically running into Bochy at games or most recently at the Major League Winter Meetings.

He was still the same guy and talking to those who know him best, many say he has never changed, which was comforting. Bruce Bochy was and still is my favorite player for a lot of reasons, mainly because his memory is something my Dad and I shared at our first baseball game together. A memory, thanks to Bochy's success, we both still get to experience even to this day.

It started when I was nine and we're still planning baseball trips 41 years later.

Tim and Henry Halloran

Team Loyalty

Growing up in Titusville, Florida, in the late 1970s and 80s, I didn't have a hometown or even "home state" baseball team to follow (No Marlins or Rays back then). So, as Floridians, we had our choice to root for any of the 26 MLB teams. In the National League, my team of choice was the hapless Atlanta Braves, the closest team to Florida but still some 500 miles away from our house. My American League team was the Kansas City Royals, somewhat influenced by my father who lived and went to high school in Overland Park, Kansas, but also by the great George Brett, whose flirtation with .400 in 1980 turned a 10-year-old into a life-long fan. That year was a turning point year for me watching baseball punctuated by Brett leading the Royals to their first American League pennant. That year also would mark the first time I attended a regular season Major League game.

It wasn't that I hadn't ever seen a Major League game — just not a regular season one. Even though we didn't have any MLB teams based in Florida, we did have spring training. Every March my dad would take my brother and me to a few spring training games a year. Sometimes, it would even be a surprise. I would be sitting in elementary school right before lunch, and the school's secretary would come on the intercom requesting the teacher to "send Timmy Halloran to the front office with his things to be checked out for an appointment." That "appointment" would be a 20-minute drive with my dad down to Cocoa, Florida, to see a Houston Astros spring training game. We'd see players from those solid 1980s Astros teams, including Nolan Ryan, J.R. Richard, Don Sutton, and Jose Cruz in the up close and personal way that those small Florida stadiums afforded.

But I didn't see a real Major League game until that magical 1980 season when Brett and the Royals were demolishing the rest of American League and I joined my dad on a summer business trip to Atlanta to see the Braves, led by Dale Murphy, Bob Horner, Chris Chambliss, and Phil Niekro face off in a series against none other than our go-to spring training team, the Houston Astros. But what I remember most about that trip was not even the baseball, but getting to experience a real city, Atlanta, for a few days with my dad.

Fast forward to the 21st century. I now live, ironically, in Atlanta with my own family, and unlike my formative years, my son has gotten to experience a number of hometown Braves regular season games. But he had also never got to experience traveling to and experiencing another big league city. That changed in 2015, when I invited my son, who, like his father, grandfather, and late great-grandfather, is an avid Kansas City Royals fan, to accompany me on a weekend trip to Kansas City in October for his 13th birthday to see his beloved Royals play in the 2015 American League Division Series. We would see game 2 of the ALDS with the Royals taking on, yes, the Houston Astros (who else?). Instead of Brett, White, and McRae, it was the stars of a new generation of Royals, Hosmer, Moustakas, and Gordon, leading the charge. In that game, we would witness the first of the Royals' record eight comeback wins in a magical run that would cumulate in their 2015 World Series championship. We also caught a foul ball, which only added to the experience. But like my trip to Atlanta, this was more than just a baseball game. My son and I experienced the city of Kansas City, visiting the Plaza, eating Kansas City Barbecue, and even seeing a Chiefs home football game. As incredible as the Royals game was, more importantly, it served as the foundation of father and son bonding, much like the experience I had in Atlanta with my dad some 35 years earlier.

It is also interesting to note that my dad, brother, and I still make a trip down to Florida every year to catch a few spring training games to see young phenoms, watch crusty veterans trying to make one more roster, and search for the ultimate sleeper for our fantasy teams. But recently, my brother and I have added two more guests to the party — our sons. Such is how the cycle of family and baseball carries on.

Connecting the Generations

Jack Herskowitz with grandson, Ryan.

When a young boy develops a passion for the game of baseball through playing and/or being a fan, the seeds of a family tradition are planted. I learned the game as a boy and played through college. To me, baseball reflects the game of life and is worthy of being a family tradition because of its inherent values.

Baseball in many respects is a microcosm and reflection of life itself. There are successes and failures in the game as there are in life. Winning the game is the goal just as achieving success in life is. There are losses and failures in the game as there are in life and one has to learn to live with both: make needed adjustments and strive to improve and win the next time. The basic keys to success in baseball as in life are practice, patience, hard work and perseverance to achieve one's desired goals.

When my son Jon was born, I rolled him a baseball which began a journey with him through high school and beyond. I coached every team he was on from T-ball through middle school and then watched him play in high school. Thereafter, we played as teammates for years on a very competitive softball team. Our deep bond was embedded through the love of the game.

The family tradition continued when my grandson, Ryan, was born. Naturally his father and grandfather introduced him to the game. I have been to most of Ryan's games and practices from the day he was old enough to pick up a bat and throw a ball. Ry is now playing baseball in high school but he still comes up to me and gives me a hug, which shows me that he is glad that I am there.

The best thing about being a grandfather of a boy playing baseball is having the opportunity to ride shotgun with him on his journey through all the inevitable ups and downs. I am a grandfather who is not living vicariously through my grandson but I am living vicariously with him. With Ry, just as with Jon, the game of baseball has bridged the years between us. Watching Ry play makes me younger again. I'm still making the plays and hitting the ball. I am made new through his passion for the game. Through him, I see the future, and through me he sees the past. My legacy and our family tradition will keep the generations connected forever.

A Lesson Learned

Rob Sheinkopf

In the early 1960s the Syracuse Chiefs held an Old Timer's Game, and my father bought tickets in advance, taking my older brother and me to MacArthur Stadium. I was probably 10 or 11 years old, and this was huge, since Dad worked 7 days a week and we very rarely got to spend time together, especially at a baseball game. We lived on Syracuse's east side of town, and Dad owned a small variety store on the west side of town, just across from the Baptist Church. Every kid in the neighborhood knew my dad as Mister Morrie, and saw him as a hero because his store was the center of their universe.

Around the 5th inning, Dad took us for a walk to get a hot dog and stretch our legs. At the concession area, we saw the great Hank Sauer signing autographs, mobbed by kids, who upon spotting my father, started yelling "It's Mister Morrie!" as they left Hank Sauer and ran for my Dad.

While they mobbed my father, I saw an opportunity to get Hank's autograph and approached a bewildered Hank Sauer who, while signing my glove, asked "Who is this Mister Morrie?"

I replied "Oh, he's nobody, he's just my Dad." Hank looked up at me, with a scowl and took me by the hand, walking toward my Dad and introduced himself. After shaking Dad's hand and mumbling something that made them both chuckle, Hank then lectured me that my father apparently was far more than a "nobody," since the kids left him to greet their real hero. I, of course, was confused (give me a break, I was 10 years old!)

I learned a valuable lesson that day thanks to Hank Sauer and got to spend a day sharing my passion for baseball with my Dad. Thanks to Hank Sauer, I understood you don't have to be a great baseball player to be a hero. I was embarrassed by the lecture from Hank in front of my father and all those kids, but I had it coming.

My parents died 6 weeks apart in 1977, both in their 50s. The Baptist Church held a memorial for them where the pastor called them 'The Great White Hope of Syracuse's west side." I had a chance to tell this story at the memorial, and several of those kids, then in their late teens, were on hand. They remembered my Dad, but I doubt very many of them could recall the great Hank Sauer.

Resources

Books

Brody, David and Henretta, James A. America: A Concise History. Bedford/St Martins. 2010.

Kirsch, George B. Baseball in Blue and Gray. Princeton University Press. 2003.

Metcalfe, Henry. A Game For All Races. Metro Books. 2000.

Miller, James and Thompson, John. Almanac of American History. National Geographic. 2007.

Neft, David S. and Neft, Michael L. and Cohen, Richard M. The Sports Encyclopedia: Baseball 2004. 24th Edition, St. Martin's Griffin.

Ritter, Lawrence S. The Glory of Their Times. Perennial. 1966.

The Baseball Encyclopedia, Eighth Edition. MacMillan Publishing Company. 1984.

Websites

Baseball Almanac. www.baseballalmanac.com